I AM AN
AMERICAN!

IS AMERICA RACIST?

SUZANNE MILLER

My Way Press

Published by My Way Press, Lawndale, CA

ISBN 978-1-7378483-0-1 (paperback)
ISBN 978-1-7378483-1-8 (eBook)
Library of Congress Control Number: 2021917954

www.suzannermiller.com

This book is dedicated to our ancestors,
who gave us the gift of life and through their labors brought
forth, sustained and passed on to us this blessed country—
truly, the land of the free and the home of the brave, a
promise for all, if each generation is faithful to that vision.

Table of Contents

PREFACE

This book is about America—how it came to be, what is special and unique about it, and what are the unresolved or newly-arising challenges it faces in the great adventure described by President Abraham Lincoln as "government of the people, by the people and for the people"[1] so that, to continue his wise words,[2] "In giving freedom to the slave, we assure freedom to the free—honorable alike in what we give, and what we preserve. We shall nobly save, or meanly lose, the last best hope of earth. Other means may succeed; this could not fail. The way is plain, peaceful, generous, just—a way which, if followed, the world will forever applaud, and God must forever bless."

Why do I use this quotation from President Lincoln to start this book?

Because I cannot imagine words of my own that say it better.

And his words quoted above address the nation of his time—a politically divided nation in which the issue of race became a dominant element of the discussion.

Now we, as a country, are in a similar place, although the current divisions may be along liberal or conservative lines. The basic issue is whether we should chuck our current constitutional system of republican democracy and replace it with a new, socialist form of government? As in 1860, the conflict is increasingly using race as its cause.

Some have asserted that the United States, from 1619 onward. was formed with racism embedded in its very structure—systemic racism. In response this book addresses a simple question: "Is the US a racist country and is that racism systemic?"

The reader can use the documented, factual information provided by this book to help them come up with their answer. I have my answer. It is summed up in three big lessons I learned from my family's involvement in American history:

1. America was not a racist country from the beginning. It was just the opposite with ethnic mixing being the usual practice rather than the exception. Racism began building slowly after the American Revolution and grew as the US economy grew, peaking in the late 1800s to early 1900s.

2. Racist oppression is driven by economic exploitation, by capitalism run amok, without humane limits put on allowable ways of making a profit.

3. The people who built America were not racists. Many were of mixed-ethnicity as well as deeply involved in opposing racism and relieving the victims of racial oppression.

I write this book not to somehow compel or trick the reader into accepting my assessments. My life experience has taught me that I am not exempt from the imperfections of humanity. Accordingly, what I write and what I say contributes nothing toward the healing of our divisions except to the degree to which my perspectives and opinions are confirmed or denied by the readers' own experience or thinking.

In the words of President Lincoln quoted earlier, this would assist us in figuring out how best to "Assure freedom to the free—honorable alike in what we give, and what we preserve.

We shall nobly save, or meanly lose, the last best hope of earth" from the lessons of history.

Why do I hope this book might help? I'm a scientist (a mathematician), and am competent at research, but I am not a historian. I realized, though, this was an advantage. Telling the history in the context of true, documentable individual stories gives what I write credibility not based on how many history degrees I possess. It also gives life to what otherwise might be viewed by some as a dreary, boring subject. Trust me, it's not— it's thrilling!

What I offer is a set of historical, documented facts, together with the thinking that led me to the three conclusions I drew from those facts. I am the living, breathing result of the people whose stories this book is built upon. By telling those stories, I can contribute to the dialogue on the issues in a different way than that of the conventional historian. These stories bring a human element into the discussion.

The motivation for this book was originally personal. About twenty years ago I was asked by members of my family to research our family's history, to see if all the old stories were really true. I found out they were. I produced a well-documented manuscript to back up the contents.

Much time passed. Then, over the space of the last year or two, I felt an unconscious urging, an intuitive hunch, to run down some stray items of information I had not previously pursued in depth. I revisited my old work but, this time, concentrated on filling out in-depth information on each individual, as was possible.

Then the surprises started to come.

The central messages of this book are derived from those surprises. What were they and why are they relevant to the current national discussion?

The first surprise was that I was racially mixed, as are a large number of other Americans. This came from my mother's side of the family. This had once been known but covered up or forgotten. My heritage on my dad's side of the family was illustrious (for the most part), and mostly British and American aristocrats. On my mom's side, I was descended from English Quakers who had been sentenced to slavery and sent against their will to the then-new colony of Barbados to be worked to death. They were tasked with clearing the island of its original tropical growth and making it into one great sugar plantation in order to provide an English source for cheap sugar for the English people to put into their tea.

What was the crime that justified such a sentence? The proclamation that "All are created equal before God."

The enormous demand for cheap labor in Barbados and the high mortality rate among workers was met by concentrated action of the part of those engaged in this English economic adventure.

My Quaker forebears were joined in their bondage by Scots prisoners of war (as a result of their defeat by the English) plus recently enslaved Black people from the West Coast of Africa. There was much ethnic intermixing in Barbados.

The ethnically mixed survivors and their offspring finally left the island and were replaced in Barbados by an all-Black West African slave force that was carefully insulated from Christian teachings. You see, the Quakers taught their fellow Black sufferers the stories of Moses and the children of Israel. There were two slave revolts in succession. The Barbados overlords were terrified they would be slain in their beds by the next one and blamed the uprisings on the Quakers as "instigators and insurrectionists."

Survivors from this group left and became the first settlers in the new colony of North Carolina. There, they were met by another ancestor of mine, a Scots prisoner of war who had been sent to Virginia instead of Barbados. He had gotten free and became a trader with the local indigenous peoples. He took a wife from among the Native Americans (Choctaw) and prospered. He obtained a sizable colonial grant of land, becoming the first person recorded as settling in the new colony. His Choctaw wife had significant land holdings of her own. When the immigrants arrived, he joined the community, helping them out with land and getting settled in the new wilderness. This is where I got the Native American part of my mixed ethnicity.

What was the second surprise? At the time, based on this effort to use tens of thousands of slaves (and use them terribly hard), the colony of Barbados became the richest, by far, of all the British colonies. *The combination of slave labor and the bounty of the land was the key to amassing great fortunes, by relying upon the desperate travail of others.* I know this kind of oppression has been (and is still being) practiced throughout the world, throughout the ages, but here it was happening on the very doorstep of America.

In summary, the oft-repeated lesson is you can gain great wealth if you bring three key elements together—a keen demand for a product (sugar to sweeten tea), the needed land or mineral resources (an entire island, Barbados), and a captive (enslaved) cheap labor force.

The composition of the slave labor force was of little concern to their overlords. Neither were the conditions of servitude. Quakers, POWs, Black individuals purchased from West Africa—the differences (including how you got them) didn't matter to the overlords. All that mattered was control of every aspect of their life and if those conditions were physically and psychologically adverse (even being worked to death) it didn't matter; a slave was a slave, a piece of property. All that mattered was the economic bottom line. You need more profit? Just work the slaves harder and get replacements to cover the excess mortality.

As I uncovered these stories and others (as I traced the details of both sides forward in time), I was thrilled by what I learned. These were wonderful people. I found they and their offspring played critical roles in the development of my country. From those stories, one could learn why particular governing choices were made in our country, and how those choices turned out.

As I traced the development of the county, I got my third surprise. I confirmed there was something unique about America—freedom. Those who survived Barbados escaped and learned how to avoid going from one oppressive system to another.

America provided a land rich in resources and benign for cultivating or capturing food (from the sea or by hunting) and it was a land with an open frontier, where one could easily gain a piece of land and be independent as well as free from oppression. If anyone tried to oppress you, you just walked away—although this took courage, the courage required of all pioneers. The survivors of Barbados also learned about shared humanity and how good religion, grounded in that shared humanity, could give you the strength to endure hardship.

In a nutshell, this was the dream of all ordinary humans—freedom and the ability to live, to meet the basic needs of both you and your family, and not live to satisfy the needs of others and to suffer (and die) from that experience. Truly, this could be, for many, the land of the free and the home of the brave. I say "many" and not "all" because in some areas of America, evil, greedy people replicated an oppressive situation. Such oppression occurred on the plantations of the South and in developing cities.

This "last best hope of earth" broke the historical pattern of oppression because of somewhat unique circumstances. A lightly populated continent with benign conditions to live and thrive and a shared experience of the founders regarding what they had been through to gain their freedom with a conviction to never let it happen again—"Liberty or death!"

This was clearly demonstrated by the Quaker founders of North Carolina. They had a distaste for oppressing others. They did their damnedest to buy up chattel slaves and others and move them to "free" areas on the frontier, eventually settling many in the New West African Republic of Liberia. In short, they were free and they had an abhorrence of slavery, in any of its forms.

This also happened in other parts of the country. Yes, there was an overwhelming demand for human laborers but it was hard to keep them from walking away. There were too many opportunities to be independent by living off the bounty of the sea, or gaining and cultivating your own land on the frontier, as the boundaries of that frontier continued to be pushed westward.

Finally, there was economic competition between those parts of the country that lived off a slavery-based plantation economy and the developing areas of yeoman farming in the Midwest. In the Midwest a person could have a family farm and, with a good-size family, produce enough to not only feed the family but also generate an excess to sell on the open market. There was a need to feed the rapidly industrializing areas of the Northeast that were less suited to farming. The problem was not producing a plentitude of crops, but getting that produce to market. The answer was the railroads. Even in the midst of the Civil War, government-funded railroad expansion continued. (Abraham Lincoln had been a railroad lawyer before he later became president. His administration contained many of his former colleagues from his railroad days.)

With the growing network of railroads (centered in Chicago) all a farmer had to do was to load up their wagon with produce and travel to the nearest railhead market, sell the produce, and return home with the money. When the Civil War began, the cities of the Northeast experienced severe food shortages. The produce they ordinarily got from the South was no longer available. There were bread riots in New York City. Eventually, produce brought in by rail from the Midwest met the demand.

After the Civil War ended there was a great recession due to an excess of products (especially produce) being on the market. Initially, the South, with its dependence on slave labor, could no longer compete without that slave labor. Only when the economic benefits produced by sharecropping took hold could the South again become competitive. This took many years to accomplish and there was an extended period of deflation (dropping prices) that continued until the 1890s. This is important because the use of sharecroppers as cheap labor was only a continuation of slavery in other terms.

The fatal fact was that the freed slaves were not given the means (primarily land) they needed to take care of themselves and thus be truly free. This undid so much of the progress against racism achieved by the sacrifices of the Civil War and enabled sharecropping.

Racism rebounded and spread because of the nation's inability to consolidate its victory over slavery.

Understand I make no claim to any benefit that comes from being white or Black or Native American. I seek no personal benefit from any group based on tribal allegiance—my native tribe is American. As a lifelong member of that tribe, I have a right to all my heritage. I do, however, draw strength and insight by honoring all the traditions of those people who strove to live, to survive, in order that I, their descendant, might be privileged to walk this earth and reap the benefits of all their work and sacrifice. I'm just me—any label someone might attempt to lay on me neither defines nor limits me.

There is a common thing that defines and unites all Americans; it's called freedom! It is her siren-song that continues to draw others to these shores. How can people not understand this? How many people of the world are clamoring to be let in at the gates from places like Russia, China, or North Korea, for example?

Our different heritages are a source of strength, not weakness, unless we fritter away that heritage by fighting each other instead of coming together as members of a human family too-long separated by the lie of racism.

INTRODUCTION

My goal for this book is to provide evidence and rationale that talks about what is uniquely American, what caused such uniqueness to develop, and how that development took place. My hope is the material gives us insight as to how to improve things going forward from the present—what things are good and should be retained while other things have had an adverse impact on our culture need to be discarded or revised and turned into positive forces for the future.

My approach in pursuing this goal is to use examples from my own family history together with presenting relevant scientific and historical evidence that will show what America, as a nation, has contributed to the world that did not previously exist. I also address what remaining shortfalls I think continue to exist and new challenges that have developed since that time.

What this book will not address is what areas might be considered for addition to the Constitution because of developments that happened outside the original context. A perfect example is the handling of the threat of nuclear war by the executive branch. What should the role of Congress be in such a situation? These are areas for new thinking.

As I pursued my research and writing, several closely intertwined topics appeared again and again—poverty, oppression, racism, and elitism—that seem to have had a dominant effect in shaping this country.

Seeking freedom from violence and oppression seems to have been a driving reason why many people came to this country (and continue to do so). Those plagues upon humanity seem to be sort of interlinked diseases of the spirit. Again and again, the desire to be free from poverty led some to form societies where wealth was extorted from others (who became the poor) to enrich the lives of an elite, which was formed and maintained to preserve that inequality.

Violence, intimidation, and manipulation (lies and trickery) were the tools used to oppress others, against their own interests, to compel them to cooperate so the elite could achieve their goals. Bad religion played no small part in convincing the oppressed that their sorry state was the will of a vengeful God, who was righteously punishing them for being who they were: poor, powerless, ignorant, and of low moral character. There was something wrong with them, they were told.

With regard to moral character, it took a couple of centuries before the Irish writer George Bernard Shaw showed us that poor moral behavior was a direct consequence of poverty. A poor person who engaged in what was commonly held to be good moral behavior (selflessness, sharing, concern for others, etc.) would result in them getting less of the goodies of life and, actually, starving in times of famine. The antidote for ignorance (which is a quality all are born with) is education, which was unavailable to them. Powerless meant they had little access to the means of power. It was the law that anyone below a certain social class was forbidden to carry a weapon, a sword.

If one of those unfortunates, by chance, escaped their fate, what kind of world would they hope for as their fantasy? A place with justice for all. Where all were recognized as equal before God, and were each given an opportunity to benefit directly from their own labor. To have the opportunity for education, to defend themselves against violence, and to guarantee their freedom by possessing the right to keep and bear arms.

This was not the dream of only the elite, but the vision of America spelled out in the founding documents of our country. There was one catch. How to achieve this?

Where nature was benign (near the water or on the frontier) those with stubborn independence and self-reliance were able to achieve their dreams. Those who do not possess those traits, however, were left in the clutches of an oppressive fate.

It took a revolution for America to free itself from the oppression of foreign elites. After that revolution, there was fear that the foreign-born elite would be replaced by an oppressive native-borne one. Great attention was given to putting safeguards in place to prevent this. This book will talk about those safeguards and how they were arrived at.

Alas, though, there was a serious flaw in the founding republic: slavery. What had held America in chains to foreign elites was the dependence of those elites upon the fruits of the earth, grown in America. To this end, they created the plantation system, where those crops could be grown on a large, profitable scale and shipped back to the home country for the great economic benefit of their elites. Where do you think all the wealth that provided the affluence needed to build and maintain those gorgeous family seats of the idle rich back in England came from?

Those elites knew a good thing when they had one. They did need a cooperative colonial elite to keep things in check. At first, these were "cadet" members of a noble family.

The English system was that the noble estates were free from taxation and could not be sold or attached for debts. This was called holding the land by entail. The problem was, the land and title to such an estate passed down from eldest son to eldest son. The girls of the family were given dowries or subsidies to help them find husbands, thus assuring them of a place in society, but the boys were all on their own after their education was finished.

They were sent into the empire to look after the family's interests. Even so, the colonial elites quickly became second-class citizens. I remember stories told about members of my family before the revolution having to deal with second-rate goods. A person in America who bought a case of glassware, for example, could be sure that it was of poor quality compared to what was directly available, at the same price, in England. Today, those are called "seconds." Even in the military, rules were in place that forbade British soldiers being placed under the command of colonials. Even so, the cadet sons found a place in the military, government, law, the church, or become a gentleman farmer, though without the protection of the entail.

There was great concern that, after the Revolution, an oppressive American elite would just take the place of the foreign one. The founding fathers of the country thought about this, also, and put additional safeguards in place.

The pre-revolutionary American elites were forced to unite with the common people or there would be no successful revolution. Thomas Jefferson was a successful member of this home-grown elite. Why would he write those wonderful words of the Declaration of Independence? That document was a sort of recruiting poster.

Patrick Henry spoke of this in his memorable "Liberty or death" speech[3], when he addressed the delusional idea some still had that they could deal with the British by soft words and submission.

> "Are fleets and armies necessary to a work of love and reconciliation? Have we shown ourselves so unwilling to be reconciled that force must be called in to win back our love? Let us not deceive ourselves, sir. These are the implements of war and subjugation; the last arguments to which kings resort. I ask gentlemen, sir, what means this martial array, if its purpose be not to force us to submission? Can gentlemen assign any other possible motive for it? Has Great Britain any enemy, in this quarter of the world, to call for all this accumulation of navies and armies? No, sir, she has none. They are meant for us: they can be meant for no other. They are sent over to bind and rivet upon us those chains which the British ministry have been so long forging. And what have we to oppose to them? Shall we try argument?... we must fight! An appeal to arms and to the God of hosts is all that is left us!"

The only way a revolution would be successful was if the British military could be countered. This meant raising an army from the common people of America. Why would a person risk his life just to get one elite replaced by another unless they were promised rewards commensurate with the risk involved? The values proclaimed in the Declaration of Independence and, eventually, the Constitution encapsulated the hopes and dreams of the ordinary American.

Once the war was won, however, what were the American elites to do? They could not oppress the very people who had just formed this incredible Continental Army that had defeated Britain's best. In no way would those soldiers allow themselves to become oppressed by a native elite. What was the answer? Slavery would continue.

Many people of color had fought in the army and they were being rewarded, to some extent, with land and, where necessary, freedom. The new immigration laws of 1790, however, forbade granting citizenship to new immigrants who were non-white.

The Black veterans weren't a problem. It was all those Black slaves on the plantations. Those plantations, and their crops of corn and wheat and then cotton, were critical to the continued success of the new republic. Both the French and British economies depended on cheap produce from those plantations to keep their own economies going.

The answer was to promote the idea that Black people were, in a sense, a different species of human being, inferior to other humans, and, therefore, needed to be ruled—to have no place in their own rule because they were inherently inferior.

How would they be "kept in their place"? By skin color. Skin color was now to be forever linked with the idea of inferiority. It could not be escaped from.

The new Constitution provided, by means of the census, and its official record of each person's race, a legal means to enforce pre-existing laws against racial mixing that had long been on the books but not easily enforced.

The long-standing practice of race mixing was now to cease. If you were racially mixed, you shut up about it.

America was converted from a society with shades of gray to one of stark black and white.

It is my opinion, based on the existing facts, that this is an important reason America is still wrestling with a race problem. The concept of race was an invention to create and maintain a permanent underclass of people—Blacks—defined by skin color. Even after the Civil War, this fiction was maintained. Race had a singular purpose—to artificially inflate the standard of living of non-Black people, at the expense of Blacks.

If this is true, an important part of any solution to American's race problem is to recognize we live in a gray world, not a black-and-white one, and end this destructive notion of race, if our country is to achieve and maintain its full measure of greatness.

This book will address this issue in these terms but, before I go further, let me now define how I will use the terms, race, ethnicity, and elite in this book.

Racism refers to the belief that human beings are different from each other in significant ways and these differences can be scientifically defined and measured. Elitism, in a sense, is a consequence of, or corollary to, racism. It is the idea that the differences between humans means that some people are superior to others, and these differences appear between groupings of people by race.

Embedded in this perspective is also the concept of racial purity. By this thinking, if you mix people racially, through intercourse, the child who results is more or less superior to one and inferior to the other racially pure parent. The idea is that humans were created as different races and each race was originally "pure." This, then, is expressed by the understanding that race has a divine mandate and mixing races is somehow sinful, in the sense of violating a divine design for humanity.

There is another term I will use in addressing these issues—ethnicity. This refers to the differences that appear between people such as language, cuisine, social principles, and, yes, skin color. The color of people's skin is determined by the latitude their forbears lived at for an extended period of time. The higher the latitude, the lighter the skin, for clear and measurable scientific and medical reasons. Actually, the other factors I mention (language, cuisine, social principles, etc.) are also driven, to a greater or lesser extent, by latitude and how long the people have lived in those spots as isolated groups.

Perfect examples of this are the modern romance languages. At the height of the Roman Empire in Europe, Latin was in common use, although each region had its own peculiar usages and accents within that common language. When the Empire in the West fell apart, people became increasingly more isolated from each other. Geographically separated groups developed in the Western part of the Hibernian peninsula. The local speech peculiarities eventually resulted in a common language—Portuguese—that was different from just Latin with a peculiar local spin. Its development from Latin can be traced as it eventually became a separate language. The same process produced French, Spanish, and Italian.

Unlike language, there is no scientific basis for race. Race, especially as defined by skin color, is a concept that only lives in the mind. Let me repeat this for emphasis. Race only exists, only has a reality, as a product of the human mind. The examples from my own family will affirm this principle. Instead, this book will show that we live in a gray world—not a black-and-white one. For a major part of America's history, ethnic mixing was quite common. A large number of "white" people living today really are of mixed ethnicity. The inverse is also true. A sizable component of the "Black" people living today is also of mixed ethnicity. Confusion about this lies at the heart of our difficulties in dealing with racism.

A final thing I'll talk about in this introduction is how I define elitism—the idea that some people are inherently superior to others. A corollary to this is that those superior people are more fit to govern the country than their inferiors. This is the antithesis of the special American perspective (spelled out in the Declaration of Independence) that all are equal and government exists to serve the will of the people. It is all the people (and only them) who have the power to define and enforce the rules by which they are governed. Any other approach results in totalitarianism and oppression.

Overview

Let me now provide an overview of what the book will cover. I'll do that starting with race, then address ethnicity, and finally summarize.

Racism

I'm telling these stories to give the reader a basis to think through a big national problem—racism. I'll start by addressing racism as a generalized topic.

The stories I'm going to tell are important because most Americans have never heard them. At present we, as a country, are deeply divided racially. The basis for such divisions is grounded in our particular history. Other countries exist that developed over the centuries and do not have our problem. We need to understand why it happened to us and not to them.

Otherwise, in my opinion, all the racial sensitivity training in the world will not get us free of this curse.

As previously mentioned, I consider the concepts of "race" to have no factual, material reality. The only reality where racism exists is in the minds of people. I will present both scientific and historical evidence of this.

First, some terms of reference. In this book, I will use the terms race and racism to refer only to the reality of the human imagination. Otherwise, I'll use the term ethnicity to refer to associations of people with some common background and characteristics.

I want to use factual historical stories and the current state of scientific knowledge to show people how alike we are. People may assume we are different and this ignorance of our common roots feeds an us-versus-them mentality—a never-ending strife of one element seeking to dominate the other. Such dominance is an impossible fantasy because of the truth I'm going to tell you.

The most powerful historical evidence I will address is this: Most Americans are racially mixed and don't know it. I didn't know it until, by chance, a couple of decades ago, when I started working on family genealogy. My mix is now a proven fact, with lots of research to back it up.

As far as science is concerned, what I write in subsequent parts of this book will present the evidence that there is no such thing in physical, measurable reality that any humans are genetically different from any other human. The only "place" where race does have a reality is in the minds of some people. This is a non-visible, non-physical reality space that is "real" only in the sense that it influences what humans say or do. Sorry, Nazis, there never was a pure Aryan white race.

What I write in this book is no sentimental stroll through the past. The things that are going to be addressed are crucial to understand if we Americans are, in the words of the late Dr. Martin Luther King, Jr., to achieve not just tolerance between disparate groups (races) but true reconciliation between long-lost members of the same family. In other words, you can't reconcile if you don't know what it is that needs reconciliation.

Let me start with the bare bones of the story. First, flat out, let me repeat to you a malicious lie that has worked its evil for generations: We humans are different—separated by race—and that you measure the degree of our difference by skin color. Each human appears to be a unique result of a roll of the genetic dice. Even so, we all come from different rolls of the same set of dice, adjusted for limited changes in features such as "kinky" hair or "protruding lips," for example.

In this way, humans are no different than doggies, for example. There are poodles and St. Bernards. The observed differences are all due to having a stable population that intermixes and becomes more suited to the locale where they live over multiple generations. In dogs this is called breeding. No matter what the breeding is, they are still dogs and can easily interbreed. Common physical traits depend on who you are related to, not what race you are a member of—whatever the word race means.

I'll devote a whole chapter to the subject of the irrationality of the concept of race.

In that chapter on such differences, I'll also address skin color—what causes it and how it relates to what race we each belong to. Simply put, skin color is a consequence of people living in a fixed geographic area for many generations. The strength of the sunlight at that locale results in evolutionary changes to the skin color of the people who live there. Skin color is very much related to health and longevity, but I'll tell you about that later. Those health and longevity issues are the result of it being evolutionarily favorable to have a skin color suited to a locale. The people who are so "colored" live longer and have healthier lives than those who are not.

Elitism

Now for elitism. There are two ways I want to address that subject. One is clearly historical. I assert that a major force that shaped America lay in a reaction by people who had been oppressed by elitism and had fled to America to escape such oppression. The second way I want to address this topic is to use evidence from both family history as well as evidence from recent events to make the same point. Also, the enemy of America and its uniqueness is not just foreign elitist oppression. Those forces are also at work within this country for an Americanized version of this curse upon humanity.

Historical and Factual Context

Let me now add some historic and genealogical details to illustrate and support previous assertions. To do so, a short summary of some of my family history is appropriate. The details will be amplified in later parts of this book.

On my dad's side I am descended (subject to some notable exceptions) from English and Scottish aristocrats. On my mom's side, I am a descendant of English Quakers, Scots prisoners of war (POWs), enslaved Blacks from West Africa, and some Native Americans.

The Quakers were arrested and jailed for the belief that all are created equal before God. Their very existence was a direct threat to the elite English class system of society and its rulers. There was a strong, different tradition regarding this among the common people. They had a saying, "When Adam cleft and Eve span, who then was the gentleman?" At one time, it is estimated[4] that over 11,000 Quakers, men, women, and children occupied the jails of London.

The Quakers opposed elitism in a scholarly, organized way, and then developed a culture that lived these beliefs. In reaction, in the early 1650s, Lord Cromwell's Puritans sentenced all the imprisoned Quakers to be sold into bondage, transported against their will as slave labor to the new colony of Barbados. This colony had been created as one vast sugar plantation to provide an English source for the sugar the English gentry needed to sweeten their tea.

The Scottish POWs were also transported in many of the same ships as additional slave labor, after the Scottish Army, loyal to the Stuart kings, was crushed at the Battle of Dunbar by Cromwell's new-style Army. Over 3,000 prisoners were captured and imprisoned in Durham cathedral[5] and about half of them died in captivity before their prison was emptied by the Barbados exile.

Other Scots followed after Lord Cromwell's armies finally subdued Ireland. Scots warriors had fought in those battles with their Irish and Welsh Celtic kin. Many were captured as POWs. It has been estimated[6] that, between the years 1652 to 1659, over 50,000 Scots were enslaved and transported to Barbados to be worked to death.

The ships from England first sailed south until they neared the West Coast of Africa, where they could pick up the favorable West winds that would take them to the Caribbean. While there, they filled out the ships to full capacity with newly enslaved Blacks. Once in Barbados, there was much intermarriage, so I also have Black heritage.

All the slaves didn't die. There were two bloody slave revolts. Many of the rulers of Barbados and their families were terrified that the next one would result in them being murdered in their beds. They blamed the revolts on the Quakers teaching the

Blacks the story of Moses and the children of Israel. They wanted to purge their slave labor force of Quaker troublemakers.

Fearing for their lives, the authorities decided on a new plan. Large-scale importation of Black slaves was begun with great care taken to keep them separate from their predecessors and their Christianity. The authorities started allowing surviving Quakers to leave. You couldn't keep them around or they would corrupt attempts to build a docile all-Black slave labor force with all their stories about "let my people go."

This was how my mother's family started coming to North Carolina. Also, surviving Scots POWs started to be freed as England gradually shook off the grip of Cromwell and his Puritans—the English monarchy was restored and the Stuart heir, Charles II, was placed on the throne. By 1679 Charles II signed an Act of Toleration that removed all the legal penalties for Quakers in his domains. A new colony had been borne as North Carolina, established by an ethnic mix of English Quakers, former Scots POWs, and West African Blacks who left Barbados. By 1820, there were no Quakers left in Barbados.

Their offspring never forgot what happened and did quite a few noteworthy things. I'll write more about that later. For now, I'll just name two of those things. First, they fought as members of General Washington's army to free themselves from their oppressors. Their motivation was remembering what the English Elite did to their people. Later, after that successful revolution, they created the first underground railway to buy slaves and move them to free territory.

Another of my forebears (on my mother's side) was another Scot (Samuel Davis) who probably arrived in the Virginia colony in the 1650s as a POW, but somehow became a trader with the Native Americans, living in the part of Southeastern

Virginia/Northeastern North Carolina covered by the "Great Dismal Swamp." That swamp was notorious as a place of refuge for escaped slaves and prisoners, as well as a refuge for Native Americans.

Samuel took a wife from the indigenous people of the country, so I am also part Native American, of the Choctaw nation, according to his will. He and his family eventually became part of the Quaker settlement in North Carolina, joining with those who arrived by way of Barbados.

When I first discovered this, I didn't realize how common this story was in that time, in that place. James A. Doan, writing on the subject in the New Hibernia Review,[7] notes, "I found that this genetic combination was actually fairly common among people I met, generally Southerners of Irish or Scotch-Irish and Indian (sic) descent." This research began with a personal interest into his own grandmother's Native American roots, with a family story similar to mine. I'll write more about this later on in the book.

Incidentally, a similar situation developed along the Georgia/Florida border where the Okefenokee swamp provided refuge for many Seminoles. In the early 1960s, during my military service, I ended up being trained in jungle survival in that area, and spent a week in the swamp doing escape and evasion while living off the land. Having been trained in the locale, I found it a veritable garden of Eden, there was so much plentiful, tasty food to be had with a minimal investment of effort needed to gather it.

I had teamed up with a young Marine from my group who did the snake part. He caught 'em and skinned 'em and I cooked 'em! Yes, it does taste just like chicken. There is a Seminole heritage center in Waycross, Georgia, that can give you more details about all this.

Let me get back, now, to personal heritage. On my dad's side, there are also some lessons to be learned. Part of me, then, comes from descendants of elitist English aristocrats who oppressed others (some out of greed, others out of ignorance). Even so, their offspring also did a few great things.

Probably the greatest thing they did was to not only turn away from becoming a governing elite themselves, but also did their utmost to create a new constitutional republic (containing almost every safeguard they could think of) to keep a new cultural elite, or a demagogue or tyrant, from replacing the British ones, especially the British King George III. Indeed, the flag of the Commonwealth of Virginia contains the motto "Sic Semper Tyrannis"—thus always to tyrants—with a symbolic tyrant king lying prostrate on the ground at the feet of Lady Liberty, with his crown at his feet.

One of my early English aristocratic forebears (Edmund Scarburgh) was a governor-general of the colony of Virginia. He was also a Cambridge graduate (Caius College), as was his son, grandfather, and brother. The latter, Charles, was knighted by King Charles II. Charles was the royal physician to both Charles II and the next two kings (James II and William) who followed.

Another of my forebears from my dad's side was clearly not a member of the elite. His name was Nicholas Granger. He was one of a group of about a hundred stray children (ages eight to sixteen) gathered up off the streets of London and placed in the Bridewell Royal Hospital to be cleaned up and sent to the new colony of Virginia in 1618 as free labor.[8] Only Nicholas and one other survived the journey and the grueling conditions into which they were placed.

Many members of my dad's family served in the military to defend their new country from foreign elitists of every stripe who wanted to either crush the American experiment in freedom and self-government or take it over to serve their own greed or lust for power.

Forebears on my dad's side served directly under Captain George Washington in the French and Indian War, and also were patriot soldiers of the Revolutionary War. One forebear, Major John Fleming, led the 1st Virginia regiment that broke the British line at the Battle of Princeton, on January 3, 1777. The British had taken Philadelphia. In desperation, Washington had to turn things around. The Battle of Princeton was that turning point. That was the first time the new Continental Army had faced British regulars and won. The world watched and took note.

Although there was opposition to the practice, many Blacks served in the Continental Army, either as free Blacks or as a contribution of their slave masters to the cause. The source of the opposition was the fear that having Blacks learn the practice of arms would allow them to successfully foment rebellion among slave brethren after the war.

In spite of this, the Elite Rhode Island Regiment of General Washington's Continental Army was all-Black. In addition, a French observer at the British surrender at Yorktown estimated that 1/3 to 1/4 of the American troops present were Black.

The reason this is so important is, after the war, lots of Revolutionary War veterans settled in the newly created Wayne Country, North Carolina, in what was then the frontier. They even named the new county for their former commander, General "Mad Anthony" Wayne. There was powerful comradery that existed there between all the veterans. The person who served alongside you would have taken a bullet for you, and you, likewise, for him, so nobody cares much what skin color you are. You are buddies for life.

There's an important lesson in this. The antidote for elitism is the recognition that we are all, indeed, equal in the eyes of God and you may be on top one day and on the bottom the next. It is the intimate personal involvement in each other's lives that dispels all false notions of race and social standing and brings about the harmony Dr. Martin Luther King, Jr. longed for.

So what does this tell us about elitism? First, that there were massive numbers of oppressed people who colonized the English colonies of America. They remembered their oppression and provided the army under General George Washington that got revenge on their former oppressors. The Declaration of Independence was, in a sense, a recruiting poster asserting the cherished beliefs of the ordinary people of America.

Second, the American Constitution, especially in its Bill of Rights, created a federal government intended to protect the common people of the country from future foreign oppression as well as to continue to provide a hostile ground to any home-grown American elitists or tyrants.

The things I have written about are not just ancient history. I assert an opening has been provided by modern political practice that has eroded the protections against native-borne elitism built into our system of government. The political practice I'm talking about is the re-definition of government policies and practices by innovative judges who are substituting their opinions in place of laws enacted by Congress, as dictated by the Constitution. This is the process being used to adapt the government to changing realities, rather than doing so by amending the Constitution. This erosion seems to me to be the same process by which the Roman Republic was abandoned and rule by power-mad Caesars put in its place.

Is this a problem now? Let me give you some concrete examples of recent trends toward an American elitism and tyranny that concern me.

Former President Barack Obama made the following remarks at a San Francisco fundraiser in April of 2008.

> "As you go into some of these small towns in Pennsylvania, and like a lot of small towns in the Midwest, the jobs have been gone now for 25 years and nothing's replaced them. And they fell through the Clinton administration, and the Bush administration, and each successive administration has said that somehow these communities are gonna regenerate and they have not. So it's not surprising then that they get bitter, they cling to guns or religion or antipathy to people who aren't like them or anti-immigrant sentiment or anti-trade sentiment as a way to explain their frustrations."

Former First Lady Hillary Clinton made similar remarks at a New York fundraiser on September 9, 2016, when she was running for president.

> "You know, to just be grossly generalistic, you could put half of Trump's supporters into what I call the basket of deplorables. Right?" Clinton said. "The racist, sexist, homophobic, xenophobic, Islamaphobic—you name it. And unfortunately there are people like that. And he has lifted them up."

I do make some allowance for the context in which these statements were made. They were soliciting funds from groups that, by any definition, were likely to be well-heeled elitists. Maybe these were not their own personal beliefs and they were just telling their audiences what they wanted to hear.

Both former President Obama and Ms. Clinton are Christians—especially Hillary, who came from solid middle-class Methodist roots.

One way or another, however, the possibility that these two political leaders may have misspoken in what they said does not change the point that they were, at the least, pitching an elitist message to wealthy, influential people who were receptive to their remarks and willing to provide substantial financial backing.

It's also not just about one or two people misspeaking. As I am writing, the governor of California, Gavin Newsom, is facing recall. There seem to be three major issues that the populace is upset about. The first is his reluctance to reopen the schools. The second is the draconian impact his shutdown orders have had in destroying small businesses, when other states have not been as severe, yet did better in COVID-19 cases. The third was the shutdown of in-person religious services, although he encountered little open opposition from most religious leaders.

The churches were received pandemic impact funding and treated as small businesses that had been forced to terminate their operation. They were being subsidized so they could hang onto their employees.

On the in-person religious service issue, he seems to be clearly acting beyond his acceptable powers, according to the usual interpretations of the California State Constitution. On the first two issues, the actions were grounded in procedures and ordinances that were not established by vote of the electorate but by the governing bureaucracy.

I have no intention of debating in this book whether those actions were justified. What seems most important, in all three topical areas, was that, in terms of public distress, the actions of the government came across as unfeeling, as if the government had become detached from the principle of knowing the needs of its people and acting in their best interest.

I know not how the recall process in California will turn out, in Governor Newsom's case, but the breaking point seemed to come after the governor was recorded on video having an expensive dinner party with political associates, and doing so while violating most of the "safe practice" protocols he, himself, had promulgated as necessary for public safety in the midst of the pandemic.

I see a lot of intellectual contempt being shared broadly in the wake of the 2020 election success of President Biden. To paraphrase, that talk seems to be: What do we do with all the people who voted for his opponent? How do we get them to see the light, to think like us?

I also note that President Biden started his administration by ruling by decree (executive order) rather than endure the will of Congress. This is dangerous. A divided Congress is reflecting a divided people. Using executive orders to circumvent Congress spells disaster, in the long run, for a constitutional republic.

You cannot have a functioning democracy if those in power hold 74 million other voters (the other half of an almost-evenly split electorate) in contempt. The essence of a republican form of government is to join together to act upon those matters where there is either common agreement or reasoned compromise, and defer acting on issues on which there are deep, almost equal, divisions.

I do not aim to make this a partisan matter. I am a lifelong democrat, but a conservative one. The difficulties I see (and are manifest in the examples I chose) are not differences of party, per se, but differences of context. All those examples occurred as a direct result of trying to govern a huge populace from the top down, by doing what you think is "good for them."

In any case, the message is clear. There are forces at work within America today that signal there is a threat to its constitutional democracy. This should be a great cause for concern to all of us.

A ruling elite that persists forever is a fantasy. Left alone, things change. There's an old saying that shirtsleeves to shirtsleeves takes three generations. Those who rise to the top on their own merit or simple good fortune have to deal with this. Their offspring are certainly born into privilege and it takes a lifetime for them to burn away all that accumulated privilege, although there are certainly exceptions. The grandchildren are the ones who go back into the common pool.

This can be prevented (or at least hindered) from happening. By the time of the grandchildren, some families will have forged a self-contained protective posture to protect the family wealth and put strong controls on who is allowed to feed from the family trough. The people involved have become so used to wealth and privilege that the idea of having to live as others do inspires feelings of terror.

I saw this firsthand when, in the 70s, I was engaged to a man whose former wife had been a member of such a family. When he met her in college, she was a free spirit but eventually reverted to type under pressure from her family. She divorced him and her family took control of the couple's two children.

They refused to let the father see the children, so he would save up money and sue for his rightful access to his children.

The family would lose the case and the court would order him to be given visiting rights. The family would let him see the children once, and then start the process of resistance all over again, using its great wealth. After all, they weren't just his children but were holders of a share of the family wealth. The family needed to bring the children up with the family mindset so they would not rebel and threaten everyone's livelihood. The stress almost broke him but the case was finally appealed to the US Supreme Court, which ruled in his favor.

The opposite outcome is also possible. If you look at the history of my dad's family, you see this principle at work. Stuff happens. My dad's family were in the shipping business but lost all their wealth in the Civil War when the major family asset, a large schooner, was confiscated by the Confederate government and paid for in what became worthless Confederate money.

As a result, the family was thrown onto its own resources to cope in the depressed postwar economy of a conquered country. My grandfather became a working man—a machinist—working with his hands to take care of his family. My own dad followed in a similar way. He ended his education after the sixth grade. Instead of going on to high school as his one of his big sisters did, he went to work to contribute to the family finances. In the midst of the Great Depression he became a shipyard worker in order to play it safe for his family after turning away from several opportunities to do other more rewarding things. To do so, however, involved the risk he would be unsuccessful and the outcome tragic.

When I came along, in the face of his strong disapproval, I took the risk. I was the only one of my siblings to go to college.

The gamble paid off. My dad was not being cruel; he was a loving, caring person. He later said some of the things he did and said to me were intended to toughen me up for the hard times of life.

In spite of this, I was privileged. The family had a strong work ethic, were religious, and were moral in their behavior toward others. Although we had no car, no telephone, and no central heating, we always had food to eat, clothes to wear, a roof over our heads, and a decent school to attend. We were expected to excel. You might say we were poor. How so? Everybody in the neighborhood was the same. That was my privilege—no psychological burden that I was inferior.

This is the beauty of America—to provide opportunity for people to take a risk and be successful. Having a rigid elitist set of rulers will destroy that characteristic of our society, as it almost destroyed that of Britain. After World War II, I remember meeting many talented British young people who told me how they were being suffocated by the British class system. They couldn't get anywhere because to do so would require the right friends, the right schools, and placement in job opportunities that were not open to them. They came to America and did well.

Racism Revisited

I'll close this overview with a short revisit and discussion regarding racism. I have already given you examples of how ethnically mixed my family is. It is not an exception.

The more I researched, the more I found out that such mixed ethnicity was extremely common in America up until recently. Most people who think they are "white," if even a part of their family has lived on this continent for a while, will usually find out they are of mixed ethnicity. The same is true of most "Black" families.

A prominent example is General Sam Houston, born in Virginia and one of the founders and first president of the Texas republic. He had a half-Cherokee wife (Scots father, Cherokee mother). He also, as a young man, spent several years living among the Cherokee and had even been adopted by one of the tribal chiefs. Many of the early families in Texas had this kind of ethnic combination. The young men were going West to seek their fortune. There weren't many white girls for them to marry and start a family with, so they married an indigenous wife instead. Many of the soldiers who fought at the Alamo were ethnically mixed or of Mexican heritage.

Now let me get down to a critical point. There is much strife these days in the US regarding racism. There are a lot of Black victims seeking acknowledgment, contrition, and compensation from white oppression. Indeed, I'm an Episcopalian, which has a heritage of being the church of a privileged white elite although some of our ministers were Black. There was a saying about them—that their job was to "comfort the afflicted and afflict the comfortable." They tended to be gifted at extracting guilt money from church parishioners who were white.

One could say they invented a game of extortion that is still being played. The game is cast as follows. The world is divided up into two groups: white and Black. Over the history of America those who are white have taken advantage of those who are Black. The prosperity of current white people is built upon the forced labor and oppression of the Black people who provided the labor. This is immoral and unjust. This historic injustice must be righted. If Black people are not paid off by reparations collected from the descendants of the immoral whites, the Blacks are justified in taking whatever they can from their white oppressors, using violence as necessary.

This argument is fallacious. It ignores a certain reality. This book will show that most people have some degree of mixed ethnicity in their heritage but may be unaware of this. Also, there seems to also be a strain of people who secretly know they are of mixed ethnicity but work to cover that up. Who deserves to be rewarded and who penalized if the world is gray, instead of black and white?

On a personal level, the dilemma I face is that I'm a product of all my ethnicity. I'm a big believer in honoring my ancestors, whoever they are. They're the reason I'm here. On a primeval level, a major purpose of each ancestor is a duty to either pass the genes along to biological children or, at least, pass along their cultural heritage to either students or adopted children. If this is done, the person is in harmony with one's own heritage. The opposite is also true. Not having biological children or students or adopted children disappoints and frustrates the great mix of all our ancestors who live within us.

In our culture, given what I've said about our ancestors living within us, if we give in to guilt, we are gray creatures living as if the world were truly binary—black or white. Such a world is one of endless strife.

If we live with such strife and have an ethnically diverse background, it disturbs the harmony of our souls. We are single indivisible creatures. Suppose I have a mixed white/Black ethnic heritage. Is part of me (the white part) to feel guilty, and the Black part to feel offended and oppressed? It is absurd. Racial reconciliation is to live as one whole person, in harmony with your entire legacy—united with your long-lost family. The challenge is not just one of justice but also one of mercy.

On a broader note, is not this the national problem of race? How do you allocate guilt and victimhood when few are purely oppressed Black victims and few are purely white oppressors? We have laws that deal with such problems on a case-by-case basis. If those laws are inadequate, let us improve and perfect them. We need to not only reconcile with our personal ethnic inheritance but also reconcile all of us who live in this country as long-lost (or ignored) siblings.

If everyone lived like that, maybe our race problem might disappear.

CHAPTER 1

SLAVES TO BARBADOS

Noteworthy takeaways:

- England created the colony of Barbados, in the Caribbean, as one great sugar plantation in order to provide the English gentry with sugar to put into their tea, at an affordable price.
- There was an intense demand for cheap labor to make all this work. The solution was to create a slave workforce that consisted of English Quakers, Scottish prisoners of war, and recently enslaved Black West Africans.
- This was a welcome solution to the English Quaker problem, where many thousands had been arrested and imprisoned out of fear that their messages of "All are equal in the sight of God" and refusal to adhere to the English class society made them a serious threat to the ruling elites.
- Working conditions in Barbados were abominable. Grueling work, a hot, humid climate, poor food and water and sickness led to a short life expectancy for the slaves. Also, existing slaves of both sexes were often force-bred to provide a cheap replacement for those who died.
- The steadfastness of the Quakers in their faith under severe oppression greatly impressed the Episcopalian Scots (who were loyal to the Stuart kings). They also taught the Black slaves the story of Moses and "let my people go." As a result,

all three groups formed a single mixed ethnicity Quaker work force.

- A succession of slave revolts, blamed on the Quakers, so frightened the rulers of Barbados that they decided to replace the workforce with a new, all-Black slave force from West Africa, strictly isolated from Christianity.

- Also, the Puritan rule of England became unpopular and was eventually overthrown. Surviving former POWs and their offspring were freed in 1660 upon the accession to the throne of the new Stuart king and, by 1679, an edict of toleration was signed that compelled freedom be given to any remaining Quaker slaves.

Here's the story. Once upon a time, in "merrie olde England," there lived a people who, through diligent research on the Christian scriptures and much prayer for discernment found themselves at odds with the prevailing religious authorities of the day—the Church of England. This was in the seventeenth century. Some of their religious conclusions were especially troublesome.

One such religious conclusion was that "all men are created equal in the eyes of God." The Church of England held a different opinion. It said that all men were created *unequal* in the eyes of God; therefore, it behooved each individual to find their proper position in the social pecking order. They were to render submission to those who were superior and look down upon those who were inferior. This doctrine of inequality was much cherished by English society of the times and justified wealth and privilege as proper and a measure of their superior status in the eyes of God. In short, left unchecked, the beliefs of these people (commonly called Quakers) threatened to undermine the entire social order of society.

The other dimension of this was that each person could (and should) be in an intimate personal relationship with God who guides their way in life and gives them strength to live that life. This was directly opposed to the Church of England doctrine of the time, which said that the Church was the vessel through which God reveals himself to humans. In colloquial terms, God spoke with the archbishop, who then spoke with the bishops and priests, who then spoke with the people.

The Quakers, instead, said things like, "What has a priest ever done for me that I couldn't do for myself?" Most Church of England clergy were well-born members of society where each member of the family took on a traditional leadership role in government, the army, the clergy, etc. Such Quaker sentiments threatened the livelihood of such clergy.

Finally, the Quakers refused to be "put down." They refused to participate in the ritual of "courtesy." Ordinarily, a person was expected to know his or her place in the grand order of society. When you met another person on the street you were expected to know if you were superior or inferior in social standing. If you were inferior, and you were a man, you tipped your hat in a gesture of submission. If you were a woman, you did a slight upright bow (curtsy). This was termed rendering the "courtesy" to your betters.

Their rebellion was symbolic but meaningful. When castigated by society for such behavior, the Quakers warned their oppressors that a righteous God would punish wrong behavior toward his children. This stuck in the face of society as a whole.

A final offense was that Quakers took the commandment "Thou shalt not kill" seriously and refused to serve in the army.

What to do? Under a succession of laws, Quakers were tried, convicted, and sentenced to imprisonment. The only proof required was an informant who testified they saw the person at a Quaker service or when a warrantless search of the home of suspected Quakers turned up Quaker-originated written material.

Soon, the jails of London were jam-packed with Quakers—men, women, and children. At its high point, it was estimated over 11,000 Quakers were jammed into the jails. Something had to be done. One of the Anglican bishops of London came up with a solution. He said, "Bondage is the solution for these heretics."

The English were hooked on drinking tea, but they had to purchase the sugar to put into the tea from foreign sources. This created a financial problem resulting in an outflow of hard coin from English banks. To solve this problem, the English crown decided to create a new colony on the Caribbean island of Barbados—to convert the entire island into one grand sugar plantation.

Where to find the labor? Growing and processing sugar cane is labor-intensive. The solution of the Anglican bishop was to sentence each Quaker to be transported against their will to the new colony. Upon arrival, the person's labor was auctioned off on the block for the best price and the profit (less transportation charges) given to the English crown.

I have read the logs of some of the ships used for this purpose. The Quaker human cargo was supplemented by the addition of Scottish prisoners of war (POWs).

The Scots came to Barbados because of two separate, disastrous events in British history. The first event was when a Scottish army engaged Oliver Cromwell's forces at the Battle of Dunbar in 1650. The battle was a disaster for the Scots—a total defeat. The Scots army was loyal to the Stuart kings. Cromwell had the Stuart King Charles I deposed and beheaded but the Scots army remained loyal to his son and heir.

A little later, in 1653, Lord Cromwell was completing the subjugation of Ireland. A large number of Scottish warriors had fought against Cromwell alongside their Celtic Irish and Welsh brethren. This produced another slug of POWs to be used as slave labor to Barbados, alongside the Quakers.

Besides my own research, there is an ample amount of confirming research and publicity as more and more people have started to discover this dark part of English history.

One of those sources is a BBC television program.[9] In it, the author, Chris Dolan, goes to Barbados and talks to a small surviving remnant of "McCluskies, Sinclairs, and Baileys" who remained on that island as well as speaking with historians. The program, "Barbado'ed: Scotland's Sugar Slaves," was described as follows, "Known as the Redlegs, they are the descendants of the Scots transported to Barbados by Cromwell after the (English) Civil War. Scottish author and broadcaster Chris Dolan went (to Barbados) to meet them to discover why they are still here 350 years later, what they know about their roots . . . Chris speaks to leading historians in Barbados and Scotland to learn how their ancestors were treated when they first arrived. Was their plight as severe as that of the black slaves from Africa?"

There's also an article in the newspaper, the Scotsman, that provides an excellent overview of this part of history.[10] An article is titled "Relatives of Scots soldiers shipped abroad in 17th Century to 'come home' and honour ancestors." The article was reporting on an event where American descendants of those shipped to Barbados after the battle came to Scotland to honor their ancestors.

Here's the gist of that article:

"Around 1,400 men were sent overseas after fighting Oliver Cromwell's troops at the Battle of Dunbar in 1650, mostly to North America and the Caribbean. They had survived capture and imprisonment at Durham Cathedral where an estimated 1,700 soldiers died of malnutrition, disease. Around 30 relatives of those who survived the battle and its aftermath will gather in East Lothian next month for a commemorative event organised by Scottish Battlefields Trust. Most will travel from the United States for the occasion. Dr Arran Johnston, director of SBT, said: 'We know about 1,400 men survived the experience at Durham. The majority of those were sent to North America or to the Caribbean and some of them were sent to fight as mercenaries in Ireland and Europe. Quite a lot of the prisoners who survived Dunbar, who were then captured, imprisoned and then given seven years servitude on the other side of the world went on and became successful, had families and created legacies. Their relatives who are due to come to Scotland are really coming back to where their family story really began.'"

The Battle of Dunbar has been described as one of the most bloody and short battles of the seventeenth century civil wars. In less than an hour, the English Parliamentarian army, under the command of Oliver Cromwell, defeated the Scottish Covenanter army who supported the claims of Charles II to the Scottish throne. By the time this battle was fought, there had been civil war in the British Isles for eleven long years, and the alliance between the English Parliamentarians and the Scottish

Covenanters had broken down (after the English executed King Charles I).

The Scots chose to support the old king's son, prompting Oliver Cromwell to invade in retaliation. On September 3, 1650, Cromwell unexpectedly attacked the larger army of General David Leslie outside the small harbor town of Dunbar and destroyed it. Most of those traveling for the event will come with the Scottish Prisoner of War Society, which has long researched those who sailed to America following the Battle of Dunbar.

Dr. Johnson said: "The society have done tremendous work in terms of finding out what happened to these people after they arrived in North America." The difficulty they have is connected to people back to Scotland. "It is very difficult to pin down where they are from as the English Parliamentarians were just not interested in keeping records. There was no effort at all to give information back to Scotland. If you were a wife or a mother and watched your loved one march off to Dunbar, you had no way of knowing if they had been killed or sent over to another country.

There are references in Kirk of Session papers of women who are later wanted to know if they can get permission to remarry and start a new life. They really did not know if they were widowed or not.

If you imagine what it must have been like for these men who, were not quite from the same glen, but would have had little experience beyond their area of Scotland, to go out and experience battle in what was probably their first military encounter."

They were then marched into England and endured these terrible conditions. And then, if they survived, to then face the prospect of crossing the ocean and beginning a new life. It must have been extremely terrifying and perhaps exhilarating. A major research project into the lives of the soldiers has been carried out at Durham University after the remains from up to 29 skeletons were found in burial pits under the city's cathedral in 2013. The face of one of the soldiers was reconstructed by specialists at John Moore University in Liverpool. Durham researchers established he was aged between 18 and 25 when he died. It was also determined he had suffered periods of poor nutrition during childhood and had lived in south west Scotland. Dr Johnson will lead the commemoration for the soldiers next month during a weekend of events planned for the weekend Friday September 13 to Sunday September 15. A re-enactment of a key part of the Battle of Dunbar will also be staged as well as a parade of mock 17th Century Scots soldiers who will march through the town as descendants of the original fighters watch on."

It should be noted that most of the Americans who attended the noted event were from Massachusetts. A portion of the Scots POWs, although intended for shipment to Barbados, ended up in Boston due to the vagaries of the prevailing winds.

This kind of thing didn't just happen to them. As will be discussed later in Chapter Four, when the English Puritan expatriates from Holland decided to move to American, they departed in two groups. One left Holland by way of England, and bought a vessel (called the Mayflower) to take them to Virginia. Instead, the prevailing winds took them to what is now Plymouth, Massachusetts. The rest of the Holland Puritans made it to their intended destination of Southeast Virginia.

I mention this here because by the 1650s, Boston was a hotbed of militant Puritanism. The Puritans there despised Quakers. Other ships sailing for Virginia, Barbados, or Jamaica with a cargo of slave labor were blown off their destination. In Boston, the Scots POWs were welcomed as forced labor and put to work in the iron works, but eventually were set free, unlike their brethren sent to Barbados. Some Quakers who were among the labor cargo were not quite so welcome.

The practice (previously mentioned) in England was to prosecute the Quakers under a succession of laws. The court-imposed punishment was for the Quaker to be transported into bondage and, only when they arrived at their destination, were they to be put on the block and sold. The Boston court records some of these Quakers were men, women, and children sold as chattel slaves, while others were actually executed for their Quaker beliefs. In Quaker tradition, these are described as the "Boston martyrs." The New England Puritans apparently supported religious freedom for themselves but not for others.

My research about Barbados and its slave labor is echoed by the Scottish blogger Elisabeth Ritchie, who lives near the area where it all happened. She covers both events, the Battle of Dunbar and the subsequent ethnic cleansing of Ireland by Cromwell in her blog post, "What were the Scots doing in Barbados and how did they get there?"[11]

She notes: "Between 1652 and 1659, around 50,000 workers were forcibly transported to the island in this way. It is said that by 1701, 21,700 forced workers out of 25,000 were of a white ethnic background. Thousands of them were Irish, many of them children between the ages of 10 and 14, kidnapped as part of the ethnic cleansing carried out by Cromwell's forces after their conquest of Ireland. Slavery and exploitation are woven into the fabric of our culture and into our greatest literature." She alludes to the writings of Charlotte Bronte, in *Jane Eyre*. "Consider poor Mrs. (Bertha) Rochester, deemed to be lascivious as well as mad because of her 'degenerate' West Indian mulatto parentage." In the book, Bertha Rochester is the mad woman locked in the attic.

In her blog, Ritchie continues, "Death rates among white 'sugar slaves', as they were called, were terrible, ill suited as they were to the rigours of the climate and suffering the same, and sometimes worse, ill treatment as their African co-slaves, who were considered more valuable. The Barbados sun, wonderful for holiday makers, is punishing to work under, especially when that work involved clearing the island of its original tropical forest. White slaves, like black slaves, suffered sexual bondage and were bred to increase the workforce, at first separately, then with Africans to produce mulatto slaves."

It is noteworthy that in 1660, when the English restoration "returned" the Stuart King Charles II to the throne, there were still surviving former Royalist soldiers who had been enslaved and sent to Barbados. Appendix B cites a surviving official record[12] where a formal Royalist officer sues the state for money to transport home thirty of his soldiers "now in slavery in Barbadoes [sic] whither they were sent by the late powers." So much for the fiction that they had not been enslaved.

All sources seem to be in agreement with my findings on the Scots enslavement stories as POWs.

Now for one final part of my Barbados heritage—the Black part.

As previously mentioned, the sailing path to Barbados was usually straight south from England until the West coast of Africa was reached. There the ships would pick up the prevailing westerly winds that blew them over the seas to the Caribbean. While in West Africa, however, the ships would stop and buy recently enslaved blacks to fill in the slots left empty by those who had died during the first part of the passage. This was deemed not as good a deal as the Quaker and Scots prisoner "free labor" as the Black slaves had to be paid for, but there was still a profit to be made and the Black slaves fed the inexhaustible demand for labor.

There were two categories of bondage—chattel slavery and indentured servitude. Theoretically, indentured servitude was slavery—but only for a fixed period of time—usually seven years. At that time, the person was supposed to be given their "freedom, a suit of clothes and a shilling." Men, women, and children were all under such indenture. Getting free was not simple.

Women who were indentured kept having their indenture extended. Something similar was true for indentured children, born in Barbados, who served for a nominal thirty-one years, although this, too, was often extended indefinitely (especially if the person was a white woman and she had borne mixed-race children). Chattel slaves were slaves forever, and all the children of an enslaved woman automatically became chattel slaves themselves.

Some English were condemned to be reduced to chattel slave status along with all their family. Others were put under indenture.

In most cases, the differences in category or ethnicity were irrelevant. The working conditions were brutal. The climate was oppressive—hot and humid—and shelter, food, and water were pitifully inadequate and unhealthy. People dropped like flies. The survival of an indentured servant (or a chattel slave) was estimated at the time as seven years, so most didn't make it to freedom—no matter what their bondage category was.

There is a credible reference to these conditions in a paper[13] profiling the Barbados colony based on analyzing the 1680 Barbados Census. Even though this time period was after the peak period of mixed-race slavery, it gives an assessment of the work environment. It notes that the wealthy planters had, "Turned their small island into an amazingly efficient sugar production machine but in doing this they had made their tropical paradise almost uninhabitable.

By crowding so many black and white laborers onto a few square miles they had aggravated health hazards, given the primitive sanitation conditions of the time and had overtaxed the food supply, condemning most inhabitants of the island to a semi-starvation diet."

By that time, the work force was being shifted from mixed to all West African Black. There was much complaining from the planters regarding the massive number of new Black slaves they had to import (and the negative impact this had on profits) to keep up with the high mortality. According to the same paper[14], the prominent planter "Edward Littleton, who owned 120 negroes in 1680 complained bitterly at having to pay £20 for each new slave. . . One of the great burdens of our lives is going to buy Negroes. But we must have them; We cannot be without them."

There is no reason to believe that real enslavement was not going on here no matter the name by which it was called, as the cited record indicates in the case of the former Scots soldiers released from slavery in 1660. (More will be said about this in Appendix B.)

Getting back to the Quakers and the English court, all a Quaker had to do to get their freedom was to go to an Anglican parish, attend a service, and get a signed note from the vicar renouncing their religion. When brought before the judge, they produced their certificate and said, "I was mistaken and mislead but have now conformed to the Church of England." This guaranteed instant freedom. Few took advantage of that possibility; they tended to hold true to their faith.

The Scots, being Stuart supporters, were Episcopalians. Even so, they were impressed by the faith of the Quakers. They watched as the Quakers held fast to their faith under extreme adversity. Many became Quakers themselves. The same happened with the Black slaves, especially the ones the Quakers taught the story of Moses and the children of Israel to. "Let my people go" was a powerful message.

Then there was the humanity issue. You never knew when you went to sleep if you would awake in the morning. Everyone—men, woman, children, Quaker, Scot, and Black—labored the same. In the night, people would reach out to each other for human comfort. It mattered that someone still recognized you as a human being and rendered affection. Many mixed-race children were born.

There were two successive slave revolts. The Quakers were blamed. A law was passed that forbade teaching Christianity to Black people. It was ignored. What further punishment was available than was not already being rendered (like torture) that wouldn't adversely impact sugar production?

Finally, in their desperation, the ruling authorities of Barbados feared for their lives. They told the Quakers, Blacks, and Scots to leave. Those people became the first settlers in the new colony of North Carolina. These people were my people on my mother's side. Many were ethnically mixed.

Back in Barbados, a completely new all-Black chattel slave work force was brought in. Great care was taken to keep them ignorant of Christianity.

This is how that part of my family first came to America.

Note: I wrote this book based on my independent research. I subsequently found there has been great public controversy about the subject of slaves sold and sent to Barbados. To dispel any concerns the reader might have as to the veracity of what I have written, Appendix B reproduces many historical records from around the time all this was going on. To me, the evidence seems convincing. I was amazed I could still find such evidence from records of the time. This is no fantasy.

CHAPTER 2

LIFE IN NEWLY COLONIZED NORTH CAROLINA

Noteworthy takeaways:

- As the political scene in England changed from Puritan rule (Lord Oliver Cromwell) back to a Stuart monarch (King Charles II), former Scottish prisoners of war who were sent by the Puritans as cheap labor to Virginia and Massachusetts were freed and took on life in the newly colonized America as traders and agents with the Indigenous people of the area.
- As white women were scarce in this frontier area, those Scots often took wives from the Europeanized "five civilized tribes"—Seminole, Choctaw, Cherokee, Chickasaw, and Creek.
- As England emerged from Puritan rule, there were two slave revolts in Barbados blamed on the Quakers. The authorities, fearing for their survival, started replacing their ethnically mixed labor force with a new, all-Black slave force from West Africa who were forbidden to learn of Christianity.
- This freed up the former Quaker slaves to leave and start a new life in the new colony of North Carolina. Once there, they were often joined by Scottish POWs who came directly to the American mainland and had become deeply involved

with the Indigenous peoples. This added a new dimension to my previous Quaker/Scots POW/Black-mixed ethnicity—Indigenous American (Choctaw).

H ere's the story.
The new settlers referred to in the introduction chapter as being from Barbados settled in the Northeast part of what is now the state of North Carolina. The first known European settlement of that area (then known as the province of Carolina) was in 1665,[15] according to an article by Martin Kelly. He notes the land had been obtained for that settlement from Indigenous peoples by individuals coming down from Albemarle, Virginia.

There is more specific information about this settlement in *The Virginia Magazine of History and Biography*. An article in that magazine[16] notes that Virginia Governor Berkeley, who was also a lord proprietor of Carolina, gave a grant for 950 acres to Samuel Davis (deed dated September 25, 1665).

Another reference[17] states that Samuel Davis, formerly of Isle of Wight County, Virginia, had come to the Pasquotank Area by 1660.

This is the first Davis I can trace in my family.

Most of my other family members moved from Barbados and settled in Perquimans Precinct, which was founded in 1668. As early as 1665, the first Friends were present in Perquimans and Pasquotank Counties on land owned by Samuel Davis.

George Fox, known as the founder of the Religious Society of Friends (the full name used to denote the Quakers), and William Edmundson, another Englishman, traveled from England to the outskirts of Hertford, North Carolina in 1672. At this time, Friends were holding meetings in private homes with conservative forms of their silent services until a formal and centralized meeting house was designated or constructed.

They settled near the water, having come in from the island colony of Barbados by ship. The earliest family names in the settlement of Perquiman's Precinct (County) were Davis, Mayo, and Clare. The Mayos were originally from Somerset County in England. Davis is a Celtic Welsh name but Clare is Scottish. Mayo is an English name from a group of English monastics who left to live in Ireland, when the indigenous English church of ancient Celtic origin was taken over by the expanding Roman Catholic hierarchy from Continental Europe in AD 664.

There was a large Mayo family presence on the island of Barbados. Although my Mayos were English (from Somerset), some family graves still exist in Barbados. An Edward Mayo was born in 1676 or 1677. His birthplace is uncertain—North Carolina or Barbados. My best guess is Barbados. Edward and Mary Clare were married at her father, Timothy's, house at Perquimans Co., North Carolina, on March 1, 1709.[18] Edward's father (of the same first name) was born in 1649 or 1650 in either Barbados or England. His wife (the younger Edward's mother) was Sarah Maggs. They were married on September 2, 1666, at Christ Church Parish, Barbados. Edward died in Perquimans County in 1700 or 1701.

William Clare (Timothy's father) was born in 1614 in either England or Scotland. He married his wife in Scotland about 1639. William Clare's father was Ambrose Clare or possibly Bogue, born about 1589 in Scotland.

All this was part of the initial presence of my mom's family in America. Soon, though, the family moved to the then-frontier area that became Wayne County as the Revolutionary War was approaching, but that's a story for the next chapter.

Getting back to the first Davis in my family history, Samuel, his land grant almost certainly overlapped land owned by the Indigenous peoples, so he would have also had to have acquired title to it from those owners. This was a habitual, fair way Quakers dealt with the Indigenous peoples.

He did so by marriage to an Indigenous woman. When Samuel died, he left a will (dated January 11, 1687/1688)[19]. That will is sealed with the great seal of the Choctaw nation, a pipe/tomahawk crossing three arrows. Figure 1 is a modern version of that seal. The Choctaws were one of the "five civilized tribes" of Indigenous peoples. Many had converted to Christianity, taken English names from the Bible, and they set up their own court system.

In his will, Samuel is recorded to have come from Albemarle precinct, which was broken into four separate precincts, of which Perquiman's was one. Samuel, supposedly, was a former Scottish POW who had made his way to the new wilderness area and had become a trader in beaver pelts with the Indigenous peoples. As the rest of my family did not arrive in the area until about 1665, it would make sense for Samuel to seek out former POWs who were living in that area. Indeed, he probably provided the land for their settlement.

The Quakers of my family were also quite active buying Black slaves and resettling them in free areas.

Figure 1: Great Seal of the Choctaw Nation

Figure 2 shows a more detailed map of the area from the Henry Mouzon map of 1775 "Published as the Act Directs May 30, 1775 at Fleet Street in London." The arrow points to the newly defined Perquiman's Precinct. Note that a substantial part of it is part of the Great Dismal Swamp—a notorious area of refuge for Native Americans and escaped slaves (and an awesome place to trap beavers for later trading of their pelts). I went there when I was young. A huge freshwater lake, Lake Drummond, is at its center.

Samuel's wife and children survived him. She was named Elizabeth, after the mother of John the Baptist and the wife of Ezekiel. For him, a Scot, to have a will with substantial land holdings in wilderness territory at such a time is noteworthy. It is almost certain that his wife, Elizabeth, was of Choctaw heritage and his land holdings were part of Choctaw lands. Until changed by settler influence, the culture was matrilineal with much of the husband's status coming from his wife.

In that society, women played a major role in oversight of the land and its cultivation. The job of the males was to become warriors, to defend the community from attack. Thus, it makes sense for Samuel's will to need assent by the tribe, as she (not he) had rights to the land.

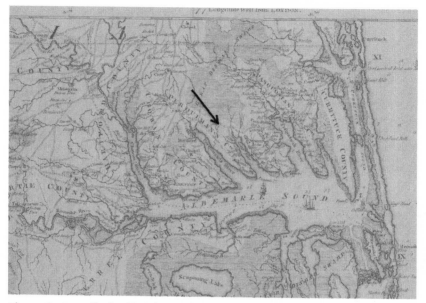

Figure 2: Detailed Official North Carolina Map of 1775

Samuel, like so many Scots settlers had probably taken an Indigenous wife because no white women were available in such an unsettled locale. Incidentally, family traditions run deep. My grandmother (from Choctaw heritage) owned the Mayo family farm—not her husband.

Among the people of that region a romantic legend developed of the Great Dismal Swamp as a place of refuge for starcrossed lovers from Indigenous and English roots. There is a lovely (but schmaltzy) poem about this. It's called "A Ballad: The Lake of the Dismal Swamp" by Thomas Moore (1779–1852). My beloved Aunt Madeleine (my dad's sister) read it to me when I was a small child.

Samuel had likely been around that area for a substantial amount of time as one of the first settlers in the wilderness area that became the new colony of North Carolina, founded in 1663, only twenty-five years before his death. Even so, he left a thriving heritage of offspring, of which I am one and provides at least one element of a thread of Indigenous people in my heritage. More will be said of other Davis family descendants in the next chapter.

When I first uncovered the story of Samuel Davis and his Choctaw wife, I did not realize the extent to which this story was common in the frontier areas of the American colonies. James E. Doan has written an informative paper on the subject in the *New Hibernia Review*. He got into this research after tracing his own family story of his grandmother, who he knew to be of "Irish and Indian (sic) descent." He writes, "I found that this genetic combination was actually fairly common among people I met, generally Southerners of Irish or Scotch-Irish and Indian descent whose ancestors came to America during the eighteenth century . . . My research also showed that the women were frequently prominent in their tribes, with the husband gaining status through the marriage and their children inheriting the best of both cultural, linguistic and socioeconomic worlds, at least until the white expansion of the early nineteenth century." Scots and Irish traders and agents, who often wrote about their experiences, were prominent among the Europeans who settled among the southeastern Indians in the eighteenth century—particularly among the Cherokees, Choctaws, Chickasaws, Creeks, and Seminoles, collectively known as the Five Civilized Nations."[20]

There is even a BBC television program[21] titled "Barbado'ed: Scotland's Sugar Slaves." The description of the program is as follows, "Known as the Redlegs, they are the descendants of the Scots transported to Barbados by Cromwell after the (English) Civil War. Scottish author and broadcaster Chris Dolan went (to

Barbados) to meet them to discover why they are still there 350 years later, what they know about their roots . . . Chris speaks to leading historians in Barbados and Scotland to learn how their ancestors were treated when they first arrived. Was their plight as severe as that of the black slaves from Africa?"

Many sources seem to be in agreement with my own findings on the Scots enslavement stories as prisoners of war.

All this was the start of the family presence in America. Soon though, as the Revolutionary War was approaching, the family moved to the then-frontier area that (toward the end of the war, in 1779) became Wayne County, North Carolina. That's the story of the next chapter of this part of the family saga.

The American Revolution and Afterwards

Noteworthy takeaways:

- There was a significant Quaker presence in the Continental Army of George Washington.
- Many former soldiers settled in Wayne County, North Carolina (named for their commanding general "Mad" Anthony Wayne). That area became an area of great tolerance on matters of race because of the ties between veterans who had served together and the strong Quaker presence there. Quite a few of these former soldiers were of mixed ethnicity or married to a person of mixed ethnicity.
- Quakers, upon their arrival in North Carolina, began buying slaves, freeing them, and resettling them into the free areas of the continent that later became Illinois, Ohio, and Indiana.
- Eventually, those same Quakers played a critical role in the settlement of the new West African Nation of Liberia. Ninety-four out of the 163 people in the manifest of the first ship carrying freed slaves to Liberia have my family last names of Outland, Davis, and Peele.

A s the winds of war approached in 1775, all my ethnicities came together in support of the colonial cause. It might surprise you that many Quakers participated in that war, but I can tell you why. To set the stage, I start with Joshua Davis, descended from the Samuel Davis mentioned in the previous chapter (and from whose wife my Indigenous Choctaw ethnicity descends). Joshua was born in Perquimans County North Carolina on December 1, 1731, and died in Wayne County.[22] In the North Carolina State Records (November 24, 1744), he is noted as receiving a royal land grant of 640 acres of land in the area of North Hanover County that was later renamed as Wayne County.

According to his will, Joshua had three sons, Richard, Joshua, and John. All three served as privates in the 10th Regiment of the North Carolina Line during the Revolutionary War. John, the youngest, is an immediate forbear of mine. It was his service that supported my membership into the Daughters of the American Revolution (DAR) after submitting hard evidence from original birth, will, and military records.

Richard was probably the oldest; he served first. He enlisted (in Wilson's company) for three years on May 15, 1777.[23] After his enlistment was up, he then served in the 1st Regiment of North Carolina State Militia according to the roster of June 2, 1780.

All three were Quakers. Richard was born in Northampton County, North Carolina, (and attended the Rich Square Quaker Meeting) according to the record of his marriage to his wife, Mary.[24]

Joshua enlisted on June 10, 1779, serving for eighteen months.[25] The other serving son, my direct forbear John, enlisted later (August 1, 1782) and also served for eighteen months.[26]

It is noteworthy that the Davis brothers served in the army even though this was problematic for them to do, as Quakers. I have traced the records and read actual transcripts from the Contentnea monthly meeting (the Quakers were meticulous record keepers).

One of those records is from early in the American Revolution. The three Davis brothers asked the meeting members to allow them to fight in the revolution without expelling them from Quaker fellowship. When asked "Why?" Their passionate reply was, "You know what the English did to our people!" The meeting voted and agreed.

All three brothers survived the war and returned home. There is a record of them attending the same Quaker meeting and asking to be embraced into full fellowship, because they were done with fighting. The meeting agreed to their request.

Another part of my Quaker heritage by way of Barbados were the Mayos. There are a significant number of Mayo tombstone and death records from Barbados about Mayos. One of them, Joshua Mayo, came to Maryland instead of North Carolina. Joshua's son, Joseph, was active in Revolutionary War matters in Anne Arundel County, Maryland.

His son Isaac, by the way, went into the Navy and was a commodore at the outbreak of the Civil War. President Lincoln offered him command of all the Union Navy, but he refused to "fight against his countrymen, and violate his oath to the Constitution." The president was furious and ordered him dismissed from the Navy rather than accept his resignation. It later took quite a bit of effort by his descendants to establish that Isaac had died (probably of a broken heart) before his dismissal papers arrived, so he was reinstated.

Isaac was not buried to prevent his grave from being des-
ecrated but there is a prominent monument to him in the US
Naval Academy Cemetery, which he helped found. James Fen-
imore Cooper, the noted author of *The Last of the Mohicans*,
knew Commodore Mayo and described him as "the bravest man
I ever met." Isaac was no racist. He headed up the US Navy's
deployed squadron in the years prior to the Civil War. Its mission was to enforce the US ban on the importation of slaves, in
conjunction with the Royal Navy (which took on the same role).
When a US warship would encounter a slave ship, they would
seize it, free all the slaves aboard it and release them into the
new US-sponsored and colonized Republic of Liberia. (Others
of my family members were instrumental in its founding, but
more on that later.)

The owners and crew of the slave ship would be tried by
maritime court. The court would order the ship sold, with the
proceeds going into the US treasury. The British used the same
process since they had outlawed slavery in 1807. They delivered
their freed slaves to their colony of Sierra Leone, just north of
Liberia.

Although the Davises and the Mayos were of Scottish and
English descent, by way of Barbados, another part of my family, from my dad's side, was Scottish and deeply involved in the
revolution. This is the Fleming part, from which my youngest
brother got his middle name.

The earliest Fleming in the line is said to have been Sir
Thomas Fleming, second son of the Earl of Wigton, according to
an old Fleming family record discussed in *Genealogy of Virginia
Families*.[27] According to that story, a Thomas Fleming was supposed to have come to Virginia in 1616, settling first in Jamestown and then moving to New Kent County. All the Flemings of

Petersburg, Virginia, of which I am descended on my dad's side of the family, are descended from him.

There is a note regarding the arms of Fleming, the Earl of Wigton in "An Ordinary of Scottish Arms."[28]

I previously mentioned Major John Fleming of the 1st Regiment of the Virginia Line in General Washington's Continental army. John was from an illustrious military family. His father was Colonel John Fleming of French and Indian War fame. Two of John's brothers served in the army—Thomas, who was colonel of the 9th Virginia Regiment of the Continental Line and William, who was colonel of the Virginia State militia.

It was Major John Fleming who led the regiment that broke the British line (and saved the revolution) at the Battle of Princeton. This occurred on January 3, 1777, after the British occupied Philadelphia, which was then the national capital. General Washington was desperate to turn the situation around or the revolution would be lost. He took his remaining army across the frozen Delaware River to try and catch the British off guard. Fortunately, this strategy worked. The Continental Army faced the British at the Battle of Princeton and was victorious, albeit at the cost of the life of Captain Fleming and many of his regiment, which was decimated in the effort.

A moving testimony to his heroism by Governor Benjamin Harrison of Virginia is reproduced in an article[29] on the Harrisons. Captain Fleming was posthumously promoted to the rank of major and his heirs received an initial grant of 5333 1/2 acres of land in recognition of his service, later supplemented by an additional 1142 acres. I mention this to emphasize the importance of the sacrifice Major Fleming and his men made to help create a new, free country. This is why, in the best of circumstances, Americans fight—to gain and maintain freedom.

You might ask what was Captain Fleming doing leading a full regiment? A regiment is usually led by a full "bird" colonel, with a set of lieutenant colonels or majors to assist him, and lead each of the battalions that compose the regiment.

The reason is grim. In the morning, this is what the officers of the regiment expected to happen. Americans had never yet been able to directly engage British soldiers and win and expected their forces to be cut to pieces by British military might; this would be the last gasp of American resistance. They had undergone months of disappointment and adversity. They just wanted to live and go home to their families and hoped the British, in the face of a failed revolution, would not hunt them down and kill them, one by one.

Those who felt this way reported in as "sick in quarters,"[30] too unwell to fight. Major Fleming was the most senior officer who did not do that. This is why he is so revered. Not only did the victory make the whole world sit up and notice, but it also gave the dejected men of the Continental Army who had survived a new hope. He and the men of the 1st Virginia gave their lives so that others might live. Without their sacrifice, the American Revolution would probably have failed.

Fast forward now to the year 2010. My nephew, Taylor Miller, the only son of my youngest brother Jesse Fleming Miller, named in honor of Major Fleming. Taylor always wanted to be a part of the military. He enlisted in the army and became a trooper in the 101st Airborne Division, serving in Afghanistan. Six weeks into his deployment, he was helping guard the major supply route from Pakistan into Afghanistan, through which all resupplies to the rebels had to flow.

He noticed a young woman close by and immediately figured it out—she was a suicide bomber. He saw her go for the bomb release and knew he was going to be a goner. In the last moments of his life, he grabbed her and enveloped her, using his body to take the full blast. By doing so he saved the lives of many around him. Only one other soldier died.

Taylor was awarded two bronze stars for his heroism. Both the Secretary of Defense Bob Gates and the Chairman of the Joint Chiefs of Staff, Admiral Mike Mullen, attended his funeral at Arlington National Cemetery. At the end, I went up to Secretary Gates and thanked him for honoring my nephew. I said, "I saw the anguish and compassion in your face as you consoled my brother. How do you do it?" He said, "If I've got the guts to sign the papers that send these young people into combat I damn well better have the guts to attend their funerals."

Many people have grown cynical and badmouth our country for what they consider its shortcomings. I tell these two stories together to remind Americans that the same spirit of courage and self-sacrifice that built this country still exists to sustain it. We have some fine leadership. Support them in the terrible demands placed upon them as they do their jobs.

Back to North Carolina. At that time, Quaker members of my family were active in promoting the "equality of all before God."

As early as 1665, the first Friends (Quakers) made their presence known in Perquimans and Pasquotank Counties. George Fox, known as the founder of the Religious Society of Friends, and William Edmundson, another Englishman, traveled from England to the outskirts of Hertford in 1672. At this time, Friends were holding meetings in private homes with conservative forms of their silent services until a formal and centralized meeting house was designated or constructed.

Another area rich in family history was Northampton County. The Cedar Grove Quaker Meeting in that county was established upon the request of Friends who wanted a meeting house close to home. Cornelius and Elijah Outland (family relatives) deeded the land on which the Cedar Grove meeting house sits. The Outlands had not come from Barbados but had come down to North Carolina from the Isle of Wight County, Virginia (as had Samuel Davis).

The Cedar Grove meeting house was situated next to a Friends schoolhouse that educated both genders. Multiple members of my family continued to be deeply involved in freeing up Black slaves and placing them beyond the reach of oppressive authorities. As early as 1768, North Carolina Quakers condemned the importation and purchase of Africans as slaves and asked members to provide moral guidance to the enslaved individuals they may have owned. Friends were far more advanced than their contemporaries of the day.

Thomas Newby of Belvidere (sic) in Perquimans County requested advice about manumitting (freeing) his slaves in 1774.

The same year of the signing of the Declaration of Independence, Newby freed ten slaves. A year later, Newby and ten other Friends freed approximately forty slaves. This drew the ire of the courts and the North Carolina General Assembly. These were precarious times with the colonists fighting against the British during the American Revolution.

In 1777, the North Carolina General Assembly took efforts to thwart the actions of the Friends toward manumission by adopting an Act to Prevent Domestic Insurrections. A portion of that law stated:

"No Negro or Mulatto Slave shall hereafter be set free, except for meritorious Services to be adjudged of and allowed by the County Court, and Licence first had and obtained thereupon. And when any Slave is or shall be set free by his or her Master or Owner otherwise than is herein before directed, it shall and may be lawful for any Free holder in this State, to apprehend and take up such Slave, and deliver him or her to the Sheriff of the County, who on receiving such Slave, shall give such Free holder a Receipt for the same; and the Sheriff shall commit all such Slaves to the Gaol of the County, there to remain until the next Court to be held for such County; and the Court of the County shall order all such confined slaves to be sold during the Term to the highest Bidder."

The United States Congress went so far as to validate and reinforce the North Carolina law with the passing of the Fugitive Slave Act of 1793.

To avoid conflict with the laws and their philosophy of life, many Friends living in Northampton County made the decision to move north and westward to free states or free-soil territories. Thus, the migration to Indiana, Ohio, and Illinois began. In some cases, Friends deeded the enslaved people they owned over to fellow Friends members and in other cases the enslaved accompanied their owners to the free territories where they were released.

This is recorded in the court records of the time. In one, the issue was the status of a freed Black slave, Turner Peele. The court found "that Robert Peele and Thomas I. Outland of Northampton County, North Carolina, being legally authorized and empowered by trustees of the yearly meeting of the Society of Friends of North Carolina take charge and convey to the States of Ohio, Indiana and Illinois, Turner Peele together with a number of other colored people held by said trustees, said Robert Peele and Thomas I. Outland having removed and placed said Turner Peele together with a number of others in Highland County, Ohio and that said Turner Peele is a free man, dated this 1st day of 12th month, 1836. Recorded 8-11-1837." Both Thomas Outland and Robert Peele are forebears of mine.

That this effort was successful is validated by the 1850 census of Fairfield, Highland County, Ohio. That document lists thirty-seven-year-old North Carolina-born Turner Peal and wife Julia A. Peal. In the 1870 census of same locale are Turner, wife Julia, and their four children.

The area of North Carolina that became Wayne County was, initially, right on the frontier.

Now, about the West African element of my ethnicity. After his service in the Revolutionary War my ancestor, John Davis, moved to Wayne County, North Carolina, and married Charity Outland.[31] She was the daughter of the Cornelius Outland mentioned earlier as a strong opponent of slavery. Cornelius, like his father Thomas, was also deeply involved in the freeing and relocation of former slaves and mixed-ethnicity Quakers to free territory where they would encounter less racism.

Incidentally, Wayne County, North Carolina, was on the western frontier of the country at that time and became a place where many Revolutionary War veterans settled after the war was over. It was a hotbed of patriots who had risked everything for freedom and equality. Indeed, the new county (like many others in the new US) was named in honor of Continental General "Mad" Anthony Wayne. He was called that for daring to oppose British regulars with volunteer colonial soldiers. Someone who had been your war buddy was not going to be dishonored because of his skin color.

I have looked into the racial makeup of John Davis' family. In the first US census of 1790 (Perquimans County, North Carolina,

Edenton District), they are listed as having a non-Native American non-white free female person as a member of the family, together with a white male head of family and two free white boys under the age of sixteen, and two free white females, of unspecified ages, but probably children. John should be about twenty-five at the time, being the youngest of the boys and having enlisted in 1782.

It turns out the free non-white female is either the mother or stepmother of John's wife, Charity. Cornelius Outland married twice. His first wife, Anna Peele, died on June 12, 1780, so the non-white person is not her. Cornelius' second wife was named Sarah Price. Their marriage is not recorded (reported married to) in the *Encyclopedia of American Quaker Genealogy*[32] until May 8, 1784. Even so, she is most certainly the free non-white female person (no age noted) from the 1790 census living with the family. Another submission to the Mormon records has her subsequently listed as the natural mother of Charity Outland and stepdaughter of Cornelius.

If Sarah is Charity's mother and is non-white, Charity should also be listed in this and subsequent census records as non-white, but that doesn't seem to be the case, depending on who Charity's father is. If Sarah is mixed-race and Charity's father is white, Charity should be a lighter, mixed-race person, who could be passed off as white.

Charity is recorded as being born on March 7, 1780, just a few months before Cornelius' first wife, Anna Peele, dies.

The likely situation is that Cornelius Outland, while still married to his wife Anna, had an intimate relationship with Sarah and she is, indeed, Charity's birth mother. This makes for a compromising situation that is resolved by pretending that Charity is the natural child of Anna Peele, born a few months before Anna died. The 1800 census lists no free non-white female living with the family but a forty-five+ free white female is now living with the family (Sarah is fifty-one at this point). She then disappears from the records. I found no record of her death.

By 1810 Cornelius is living with his son Exum Outland and his family in Indiana, and is eventually buried there.

In all probability, John's wife Charity is mixed-race and her mother (Cornelius' second wife) was free Black or mixed-race. These are the two Black forbears I have so far traced. I still do not know who the parents of Sarah are, although she is said to have been born in Wayne County.

There is additional support for a cover-up. A key page of the 1800 Wayne County census records was damaged. Starting that year, the list of information in the census records was expanded and ages were recorded for all free white persons, both male and female. Unfortunately, the upper right-hand part of that page containing the information has been cut off. This was the part of the record that contained the age data only for the family members of John Davis and that of his brother, Joshua. What a strange coincidence? Altering an official federal record is a felony. With the missing data, it was easier to pass off Cornelius' second wife as not existing. It is fortunate that I was able to recover the missing information from other sources.

Now for an amazingly good side of the Outlands. As previously mentioned, Charity's father, Cornelius Outland, was a leader of the North Carolina Quaker community. There are records of him and his father, Thomas, representing that community before the courts in arranging for the manumission (freeing) of Black chattel slaves and resettling them in new lives in what is now Ohio, Indiana, and Illinois. This is why census records for members of his family have significant numbers of slaves in their households.

Nowadays the Outland name is mostly found in only two places[33]—the US (2319 times) and Liberia, West Africa (350 times). This is due to the Outland family's history of being involved in freeing and resettling Americans of color in safe areas. Liberia was one of those areas. It was established in 1821 on land acquired for free and recently freed Blacks by the American Colonization Society.

I found two important blog posts on this subject. The first,[34] "50 Shades of Grey and Counting," is written by an ethnically mixed person who found 20 percent of his DNA is Swedish through his mother and the North Carolina Quakers this section of the book is about.

The second,[35] "5 thoughts on Me, Quaker manumissions—and an 1828 voyage to Liberia" is also important. The latter blog documents the voyage of the brig Nautilus from Hampton Roads, Virginia, in 1828, carrying a large number of colonists to the new country of Liberia. This post clearly documents names and other personal information about a large number of people with the Outland surname and also a great many people with other surnames of my family—Davis and Peele.

There is a lot to sort out here. Obviously, many slaves took on the English last names of their owners, but some may also be ethnically mixed family descendants who moved to Liberia. Which of the settlers has what ethnic mix? The Outlands, Davis', and Peels were active in the buying up and resettling of slaves, so that blog post lists the records of a large number of people with the same last names. Out of the 163 people named in the ship's manifest for resettlement, ninety-four have one of my three family names.

The connection between the Outlands, Davis', Peeles, and me comes from a child (born 1811) of John Davis and Charity Outland—my great-great-grandmother, Celia Davis. She and my great-great-grandfather were married in one of the Quaker meeting houses in Wayne County.

After the Civil War, there were no longer any Quakers in that area of North Carolina. Their numbers began dwindling after the Revolutionary War. Some left the area. Many Quakers married former Episcopalians after the demise of that church as a consequence of the revolution and, as a compromise, started attending services in the newly emerging Baptist church.

Another factor was the prosperity that stemmed from farming. You needed slaves to work the fields and some affluent family members who remained in the state may have become slaveholders or married slaveholders, which was incompatible with a Quaker heritage. Although the former Quaker meeting house at Nahunta (then called the Contentnea meeting) was closed in 1851, it still stands. Today, it is a little country Baptist church.

CHAPTER 4

HOW WE GOT OUR REPUBLICAN FORM OF GOVERNMENT—MY DAD'S SIDE OF THE FAMILY

Noteworthy takeaways:

- At the end of the Revolution, America almost became a monarchy instead of a republic. The founding fathers were leery of pure democracies. They reviewed history. Throughout history, America's founders saw the problems democracies had in sustaining themselves. Once it was clear America would not become a monarchy, they wrote the Constitution and built in many constraints to deliberately hinder the potential takeover of the republic by elitist groups and tyrants, as had always happened before in history.
- There were two sets of Pilgrims who came to America, although they were originally a single group of English expatriates living in Holland. One set was blown off course and their ship, the *Mayflower*, landed at Plymouth Rock, Massachusetts. The other group made it to their planned destination, Southeastern Virginia.
- The Southeastern Virginia group was expelled by the royal governor for refusing to conform to the Church of England. Instead, they accepted an invitation from Lord Baltimore to

resettle in his new domain of Maryland. They founded Anne Arundel County and the city of Annapolis.

- After zealous pursuit of their own religious liberty, the Boston group tried and sentenced Quakers there to both degradation into chattel slavery and killed others for the sin of heresy—believing that one could have a personal relationship with God. In Quaker tradition, they are called the Boston martyrs.

- The leader of the Southeast Virginia group of Puritans was sent with an armed force to bring the colonies of Virginia and Maryland (who were loyal to the Stuart kings) into subjugation to Cromwell's Parliament. The leader did so by offering them a charter of rights in exchange for their submission.

- This early history of our country shows how difficult (and objectionable to those ruled) it is to have a ruling elite in control of the government. The usual way such an elite was maintained was through the oppression of others. Otherwise, those on top usually eventually find themselves on the bottom, and learn a little humility.

As previously mentioned, my dad's family came from British aristocratic stock, and an inter-related set of family members held (and continued to hold) positions of privilege in America for a long while. There was one colonial governor (Richard Bennett of Virginia), Henry Bagwell the first clerk of courts of the new county of Accomack in Virginia and an early and long-term member of the House of Burgesses (the governing body of the Virginia colony), a governor-general of Virginia (Edmund Scarburgh), many other members of the House of Burgesses, the first president of the Continental Congress (Peyton Randolph), four US presidents. (Washington,

Madison, Jefferson, Zachary Taylor), and more. The families expanded their positions into the colony of Maryland.

Let's start from the beginning in Virginia. Although Virginia was settled in 1607, the earliest member of my family in America was Henry Bagwell. He came to Virginia in 1610, having been delayed when in 1609 his ship, the *Sea Venture*, carrying the second wave of colonists, sailed right into a hurricane. The survivors were washed up on the shore of Bermuda, together with what was left of their ship. The story was the basis for Shakespeare's play, *The Tempest*. It was touch and go. There is no natural water supply on Bermuda. There were also no trees.

Even so, after sorting things out they had a plan. They used all the wood they could salvage from the wreck to build a small ship, the *Deliverance*. They used this ship to take them off the island and land them safely in Virginia.

Another early part of the family descended from some fervent Stuart supporters in England. They were Scarburghs from Norfolk, England. The family was prominent for centuries in British history. It can be traced back to 914, to the Viking stronghold of Dalby, on the Isle of Man. Being somewhat warlike, the family distinguished itself in the crusades. Indeed, the family coat of arms has a lion holding a spear upon which a Saracen head is impaled.

I'll start with a Henry Scarburgh. He was a Cambridge graduate (Caius College), as were two of his grandsons, Edmund and Charles, and Edmund's son (also named Edmund). Edmund appears in the Virginia colony by 1620 or 1621. Edmund's brother Charles, after attending school at Cambridge (and leaving with a reputation as a gifted mathematician), went to Oxford, gained a medical degree, and became the court physician to Charles

II, James I of England, and King William of Orange. He was knighted by King Charles II.

Edmund managed the family's interests in Virginia. His son married Elizabeth Bennett, the daughter of another person (and family) prominent in Virginia history, Richard Bennett. Edmund was given a grant of land from King Charles II for 7950 acres. A sizable part of this grant was entailed and, therefore, not taxable nor subject to attachment for debt and passed from first son to first son in every generation. Incidentally, one of the first acts of new Virginia Council of 1776 was to eliminate this practice of entail, although not every state followed. This was one of the practices that, in England, sustained a ruling elite.

I've mentioned all the preceding information for one purpose: to give the reader the background for a pivotal event in US history that most people know nothing about.

After the successful American Revolution, the founding fathers were intent upon discarding the previous governing document, the Articles of Confederation. That agreement had been a temporary measure to allow the separate colonies to unite to oppose the British and prosecute the war, then replace it with a more permanent government structure.

Large number of Scots had come to this country as a consequence of their loyalty to the Stuart royal line. This was understandable as the only government connection between the colonies and Britain had been a common king. The American colonies were an entirely separate, private business activity undertaken by the Stuart kings, and had nothing to do with Parliament. Parliament was an institution solely designed for the government of England.

In that context, Virginia (and most of my dad's family) continued its loyalty to the Stuarts. The British tyrant they fought, George III, had not a drop of Stuart blood.

After substantial deliberation, in 1782 a set of people was empowered by the Continental Congress and the president of that congress to go to Italy and offer the "kingship of America" to Charles Stuart, "Bonnie Prince Charlie," the son of James Francis Edward Stuart (styled the "Old Pretender") who was the son of the deposed King James II of England.

Charles Stuart had lost the family cause with the British defeat of the Scots at the Battle of Culloden. Being Catholic, he was living in Rome under the protection and support of the pope. Charles Stuart's father, James Francis, at the death of his sister, Queen Anne, was denied the throne because he was a Catholic. Instead, the British government installed the German prince, George I of Hanover.

Prince Charlie demurred. He said he might have considered the American offer if he were younger (he was in his sixties at the time). He died in 1788. But for that, the US, instead of a being governed by a written constitution, might have become a kingdom on the Scottish model, governed by a Stuart king and his descendants. Why did they act this way? They looked back in history and how all previous democracies had become dictatorships through manipulation by a demagogue.

The Roman republic was abolished by Julius Caesar manipulating the mob and using his command of the legions to intimidate the governing body, the senate. Previously, the senate had placed careful control on how much power might be given to an individual, and under what circumstances? Through his manipulation and exploitation of serious crises Caesar forced the senate to vote for him to have "dictator" powers. One gained, he never relinquished them and used the legions to subdue his opponents.

The greatest fear of the writers of the US Constitution was that, in either a full democracy or republic, voters might be manipulated by a demagogue so he could gain power, like Caesar. Their solution to controlling this concern was the Electoral College, where individual electors could use their own judgment and take the initiative to block a demagogue from power. This is why the power-hungry are always proposing the elimination of the Electoral College, even though, it could be argued, it has become irrelevant. It would be difficult to envision an "independent override" of a popular vote, without provoking massive discord and violence.

Let's get back to my family history. Another prominent part of my dad's family were the Bennetts. The Bennetts were officers of the Virginia Company, the company that first settled Virginia in 1607. Initially, it was a private business venture of the English king, run by its stockholders. It was only in 1628, after the colony became prosperous, that King Charles I took over the direct governance of this new colony.

Before that, the Bennett family played an important part in English history. They were originally Puritans, people who wanted to reform the Church of England in a more pious direction. This put them at risk of persecution by the English authorities of the time, so they went into exile in the Netherlands so they could worship and live as they pleased.

In Amsterdam, the Dutch government gave the group of English exiles an old church to use for their worship. It had originally been the church of the Catholic Beguines, a group of lay sisters with a tradition of devoting the early part of their life to serving others. It had been confiscated by the Dutch government as part of the Reformation. The Beguines were placed in, or assigned to, various families to provide needed care. This service was only for a limited time, however. After a few years of service, such young women usually married and formed a family of their own. The populace prized them as potential wives.

The Puritan community formed around that church. It still stands (listed as the Ancient Church of the Pilgrims) under the governance of the European authorities of the Presbyterian Church. Instead of having a bishop, the community was led by a ruling elder. He was one of my family's forbears, Edward Bennett.

There was a favorite bar near the church where the community often gathered. The bar owner was named John Custis. He married into the Bennett family and it was a widow of one of his descendants, Martha Custis (born Martha Dandridge), who married George Washington and provided him his fortune from what was originally Bennett wealth.

There was eventually religious strife within this community of English expatriates. I was told that the major difference was whether to be what we would call today liberal or conservative in matters of church reform. The difference was more in the severity with which deviation from doctrine was punished. Eventually, the church community split over this issue. At the same time, the Eastern part of North America was becoming settled.

The more conservative group went back to England for a short time during which they acquired the *Mayflower* and set sail for the new world. Their original goal was to settle in Virginia but somehow (either because of the winds or some other reason not apparent) they landed instead at Plymouth Rock.

They became known to posterity as the Massachusetts Pilgrims. They were the forbears, religiously, of the Congregationalists.

Coincidentally, the Boston church was the group that executed some Quakers (and condemned others to chattel slavery) there. The zeal of the New England Puritans for religious freedom did not extend to others.

The more liberal element also went to the new world, but settled in the original target—Southeast Virginia.

Then troubles hit. In 1628 there was a concerted attack by indigenous people on the Southeast Virginia colonists that greatly diminished their number. Then the group came under attack from the Virginia government.

The northern Puritans established Harvard College to be a seminary to train Puritan ministers. The Virginia group of colonists asked the head of the new institution to provide several pastors from the college to serve the people of Southeast Virginia.

When the royal governor of Virginia, Lord Berkeley, found out about this, he reacted strongly and swiftly. He issued an edict that the Virginia Puritans either conform to the Church of England or leave Virginia. He gave them a year to do this.

Fortunately, the English king's foreign minister, Lord Baltimore, had been granted his own fiefdom in America. It was called Maryland and was carved out of the northern part of the Virginia Colony. Lord Baltimore was king in everything but name only. Apparently King Charles I was worried about providing a place of refuge for his family and other English Catholics (especially because his queen, Henrietta Marie, was French and Catholic). Maryland was supposed to be that refuge.

Lord Baltimore was having trouble recruiting settlers for Maryland. The king had previously designated Newfoundland (in what is now called Canada) as his first choice for a refuge, but living conditions were so severe there nobody would emigrate. They had even named this first colony Avalon, to make it sound appealing, but there was little soil—mostly rocks, with a few trees growing out of crannies in the rocks. Maryland was his second shot. This is why settlers were so wary of immigrating to Maryland.

Lord Baltimore found out about the banishment of the Virginia Puritans from his brother, Leonard, who was serving as governor of Maryland, and offered them land and a guarantee of religious tolerance if they moved to Maryland. They agreed. In 1648, they founded both Anne Arundel County and what is now the city of Annapolis (then named Providence). A direct forbear of mine, a nephew of Edward Bennett named Richard Bennett, led followers up to Maryland.

I had another part of my family already settled there at what is now the Aberdeen, Maryland, Army proving grounds. The man's name was Nathaniel Utie. His plantation was called Spesutie (the home of Utie). Nathaniel had a son (also named Nathaniel). After the elder Nathaniel died, his widow, Mary Ann Utie, remarried to Richard Bennett's son (let's call him Richard II). She produced another son, Richard Bennett III. Both Richard III and his stepbrother, Nathaniel Utie II, were members of the first class of students at the newly founded Harvard College.

Then the Puritan revolution hit England. The new "roundhead" Parliament heard that the colonies of both Maryland and Virginia were still loyal to the Stuarts and decided to do a power grab, now that England no longer had a king. This is where the name "Old Dominion" for Virginia comes from. Later, when the son of Charles I, Charles II, was put onto the throne of England, he often referred to Virginia as "my old dominion."

In 1651 Richard Bennett, together with two other Puritan loyalists, were provided with some ships and troops to sail to America and "force those colonies to submit to the authority of parliament."

Richard Bennett sailed first to "James Cittee" (what Jamestown was then called), the capital of the Virginia colony and stood his ships offshore with gun ports open while he went ashore to discuss the matter with the Colonial Assembly.

Purportedly, Richard told them that Parliament had heard rumors the Virginia colony was still loyal to the Stuart "pretender" king. He is said to have told them he hoped this was not true because, if it were, his orders were to use those guns to blast the town to smithereens and then put the troops ashore to arrest anyone they found to still be alive.

Supposedly, the citizens asked how they might prove their loyalty to Parliament. Richard replied that he had drafted an agreement to that effect and all that was needed was for all the assembly members to line up and sign the document. The gentry asked if they could be granted some benefits for so doing to show their fellow colonists (whose interest they were supposed to represent) they didn't just cravenly submit.

Richard is said to have seen the wisdom in that request and drew up a list of rights he said Parliament had authorized him to grant to help pacify the colony. Thomas Jefferson provides a copy of that agreement in his book *Notes on the State of Virginia*. The colonists got a lot in the deal, so everybody signed the document of submission.

Richard and his company then went back on board and sailed to St. Mary's City, the capital of the Maryland colony, and repeated the process with the same results.

Richard then returned to Virginia and informed Lord Berkeley that Parliament was removing him as governor of the colony; Richard Bennett would become the new governor.

It is noteworthy that Thomas Jefferson, in *Notes on the State of Virginia*, referred to this document as evidence that the British were totally untrustworthy. They (either the king or Parliament) had, over the years, violated every one of those binding legal promises from Parliament.

This is how we came to have a specific written Constitution, unchangeable except by a rigorous process of affirmation by the people. Without such a document of this type (and a Supreme Court whose major purpose is to serve as a check on both Congress and the executive branch), the country would be vulnerable to the gradual erosion of rights by executive (King) and Congress (Parliament) they had observed happen in England, or power could be directly seized in a coup.

Note the long, tedious process it took to produce (or amend) that document. It was forged from the cumulative experience of people fleeing persecution and then coming into conflict and shedding blood to retain those rights. People had learned a hard truth that the one who is on top today may be on the bottom tomorrow, and thus it behooves us to be gentle with one another in our disagreements. Without a system of checks and balances that are effective, over time elite-controlled governments and tyrants will tend to chip away at the rights of its citizens.

I'll add one more note to this chapter about what the fathers of our republic succeeded in doing. Establish a promised land for all, in some locales and for some time.

I'll talk specifically about the Eastern Shore of Virginia. In my genealogy activities I came across the 1860 federal census for Accomack County, Virginia, the northernmost county on that peninsula. Up until even the 1960s it was an isolated area. Nobody went there unless you intended to, until a bridge was built connecting the tip of that peninsula to Southeastern Virginia.

In 1860, just before the Civil War, the population of that county was heavily Black with only a small number of those being slaves. Freed Black slaves had gone there to live after their manumission. On a whim, I wrote down a list of occupations mentioned in the census and then went through that list, by color. I discovered something interesting. The percentage of people in a given occupational category (cake baker, lawyer, farmer, waterman, etc.) was almost identical, regardless of race.

Why was this so? Well, if you had any kind of useful trade, you could get paid for your work. You could save up your wages and eventually buy a small plot of land. You could then, with the help of friends and neighbors, build a small house. The climate was temperate. You could plant a garden and bring in two crops per year. The wife could preserve a lot of the garden's bounty for the short winter. Once again, with the support of friends and neighbors, you could all get together and build a boat. The community could then use the boat to bring in a bounty of fresh seafood from the Chesapeake Bay to share. You didn't have to even work at your trade for very long—maybe a few months a year to bring in a little cash money.

From my visits to family there, I observed how talented the people were. My uncle Emerson did a great job of building superb replicas of boats and ships and selling them. He was also good at carpentry and drywall.

I was told that in the 1920s, hotels wanted to move into the area to take advantage of the temperate climate and the fresh food, especially seafood. They failed. Nobody was willing to staff the hotels for the meager wages they offered when you could do much better at something you liked to do and that other people found to be valuable.

Although there were said to be some racist areas, I never noticed any noteworthy racism—no "separate but equal" fantasy. Everybody was sort of the same, regardless of skin color. The people were also pious. I went to the little pre-Revolution Episcopal church (St. George's Pungoteague) that was a traditional place of family worship. It was built in the form of a Greek cross, but the Union army occupied the Eastern Shore during the Civil War and used the church as a stable for their horses. They burned the wooden pews and altar as firewood. They were going to teach these stubborn rebels a little humility.

"Stubborn rebels"? The area was loyal to the Union throughout the war. The county representatives voted against secession every time it came up for a vote. The local courts continued to function. These were gentle, God-fearing people. After the war, there was great debate by the federal government to make the two counties of the Eastern shore of Virginia into a separate state, like they did (unconstitutionally) with West Virginia, but they eventually decided not to.

After the occupation ended, the people came together to rebuild what had been destroyed. Only one arm of the Greek cross was reparable, so that's what the rebuilt church consists of today.

I started to realize what a breath of fresh air it must have been like for someone fleeing persecution to come here.

What I write about on the Eastern Shore must have been similar to what happened in the frontier areas of the country. The cities were probably a mess, but after you paid off the cost of your passage, you could take your young family and go west.

You'd get your own piece of land to farm, and get the protein the family needed by hunting from a plentiful supply of game.

I remember my grandparents and their farm in North Carolina. They were self-sufficient, only needing to go into town once or twice a year to buy things like sugar and salt and flour. Most of the time, though, we would eat cornbread, made from the corn they grew on the farm or hams that had been smoke-cured for preservation, or chicken and turkey. We made our own butter and cheese.

Have we ruined ourselves and the American dream by being greedy? I remember thinking, "When do we cease to own the stuff and it begins to own us?" I remember getting divorced after twenty years of marriage and going from a four-level "palace" of a house in the Maryland suburbs to an efficiency apartment in Alexandria, Virginia. I walked in the door and started crying. After all these years of work, this is all I've got? I then stopped crying and started laughing. I realized how free I was of the burden of dragging around all that previous stuff on my back.

Let us all work together and figure out how to, once again, give people the opportunity to be free and independent, to free them from the burden of having to become a paycheck factory for their debtors.

CHAPTER 5

RELIGIOUS LIBERTY

Noteworthy takeaways:

- It is difficult to underestimate how important the ability to practice one's religion, free from oppression, was in motivating immigrants to undertake the perilous voyage and resettlement in America. This produced a great variety of religious practice. Here's the rundown of the initial religious orientation of each colony:
  - Massachusetts and Connecticut: Puritan
  - Maryland: Roman Catholic
  - Virginia, North Carolina, South Carolina, Georgia: Church of England
  - New York, New Jersey, Pennsylvania, Delaware: No dominant religion
  - New Hampshire: No dominant religion
  - Rhode Island: Nonconformist
- A major group of settlers were the Puritans exiled from Holland—people who felt the English Reformation from English Catholic to Church of England did not go far enough in cleansing the religion from papism.

  There were two major settlements of Puritans—one that landed at Plymouth Rock and founded the colony of Massachusetts and another that initially settled in Southeast Virginia but were expelled by the royal governor of Virginia for not submitting to the Church of England. This group resettled to Maryland, at the invitation of Lord Baltimore and founded a city originally named Providence, but later renamed Annapolis, and Anne Arundel County.

- The Massachusetts Puritans became religious oppressors.
  - Trying and executing some Quakers and condemning others (men, women, and children), to chattel slavery
  - Persecuting non-conforming members of their original group of settlers who, under the leadership of Roger Williams, left and founded the new religiously-free colony of Rhode Island
- After getting settled, the English Civil War began and the Maryland Puritans overthrew Lord Baltimore at the battle of the Severn in 1655 (the only part of the English Civil War fought on American soil). They then assumed control of the government, and submitted the colony to the authority of the English Puritans under Oliver Cromwell, who had arrested and executed King Charles I.
- The same thing happened in Virginia. The colony submitted to the authority of the Puritan Parliament and the royal governor was replaced by a Puritan governor, Richard Bennett, a direct forbear of mine.
- After the Puritans in England were overthrown and King Charles II placed on the English throne, the same royal governor in Virginia was returned to power peacefully and Lord Baltimore's province was restored to the family under the condition he convert to the Church of England.
- All these battles of "who's on top today," religiously, finally got through to the colonists. Gradually, the Protestant form of their religions became tolerant. This tolerance became a specific right under the new American Constitution and

eventually the last two states disestablished the Puritan Congregational Church, Connecticut in 1818 and Massachusetts in 1833.

- Under the Constitution, originally, each state was in charge of religious matters. This principle was revised in 1940 (in Cantwell v. Connecticut) by the US Supreme Court asserting that the due process clause of the Fourteenth Amendment meant that state law in this area was now subordinate to federal law. That federal law is terse. The specifics with regard to the federal government are to not establish a single religion at the federal level and not meddle in church matters, but to guarantee all citizens freedom of conscience—and forbid any personal penalty based on a person's religious orientation.

I covered some of this material and family information in Chapter 3 and aim not to repeat, but to amplify that material with a specific focus on religion.

As previously mentioned, a key driver that brought people to America was freedom from oppression. People wanted to live their lives without the government telling them what to do.

There was a strong religious element in this. A major force behind the creation of America as we know it was the urge for freedom in one particular area—religion.

Up until the founding of America, religion had been looked upon as part of the government—reporting directly to a king or emperor. Each ruler had a group of religious supporters who pledged their personal allegiance to him. There is a saying from one of the Roman emperors about this: In time of peace I rule through the church, in time of war I rule through the legions.

King James I of England said something similar, "no kirk, no king."

This is the way it was in England. There was an established religion—the Church of England—that was sustained by tax money. The clergy took a personal oath to support the king. The people, in every Church of England parish in the world, prayed specifically for him. Unfortunately, this was a one-size-fits-all kind of thing, with an established common belief system that all were expected to subscribe to or, otherwise, suffer penalties. In England, this included being forbidden to serve in the government or in particular professions if you were not Church of England.

The Church of England was spun off from the English Catholic church by the English Reformation. The Puritans said the reforms did not go far enough. Others (such as the Quakers) felt that even the Puritans did not go far enough and preached and lived a doctrine of "all are equal in the eyes of God," which attacked the social order of England. Under that doctrine people were unequal, some inferior, and the persons of privilege were so because God approved of them and disapproved of others. The role of the inferiors was to serve the elite. In addition, all were expected to pay taxes to support the established church, regardless of your personal beliefs.

The Puritans wanted the freedom to form their own society and worship God in their preferred way.

The Quakers felt likewise, except added a refusal to submit to a church hierarchy as the only channel through which people could receive God's guidance. They were tried and convicted in an English church court for believing that a person could have a personal relationship with the divine and that all were equal. Their punishment was to be enslaved and transported against their will to a foreign land to have their labor sold on the block, whereupon they would be worked to death.

Unfortunately, Quakers were not welcome in the Massachusetts colony. When Quakers there refused to recant their beliefs, the Boston Puritans executed some and passed a law authorizing the sale of whole families of others into chattel slavery.

There were also some dissenters from the kind of Puritanism practiced in the Massachusetts colony. Some of the more liberal members of that colony left and, under the leadership of Roger Williams, formed their own colony of Rhode Island—in many ways, it was the first Baptist colony.

In addition, the governor of the Virginia colony exiled Puritans who had settled into Southeastern Virginia, unless they submitted to the Church of England, the established religion of that colony. In 1649, those Quakers obtained an agreement from the governor of the colony of Maryland (Lord Baltimore's brother, Leonard) to have them move to Maryland where they would be granted land and religious tolerance.

Maryland had learned its own lesson. King Charles I was rumored to be a secret Catholic. His wife, Henrietta Marie, was a French princess and was Catholic. There was great religious unrest in England as various members of the House of Stuart became king or queen. The country had seesawed back and forth with public executions as power shifted one way or the other as the country itself had gradually become Protestant.

Queen Elizabeth was in danger before she assumed the throne but, once installed as queen, had her own cousin, Mary, Queen of Scots, executed. Charles feared for his own life and that of his family so he arranged with his foreign minister, George Calvert, the first Lord Baltimore, to establish a place of refuge in America for his family and English Catholics should the need arise for such a place.

Initially, King Charles gave Lord Baltimore the province of Nova Scotia (now part of Canada), but it was a cold barren place, and Lord Baltimore couldn't get enough settlers. The king then carved out the northern part of Virginia, and gave it to Lord Baltimore, calling it Maryland. Jesuit clergy established the new colony. After a while, the Maryland Jesuits began speculating in land, to the great financial benefit of their order. Fortunately, the Vatican got wind of this and stopped them. The Vatican did not want to have this new place of refuge ruined by well-intended (but not well thought out) Jesuit shenanigans. Unlike the other colonies, however, King Charles had made Lord Baltimore king of that territory in everything but name. Lord Baltimore had vast powers, but he had trouble getting people to settle there because word got around about the Nova Scotia situation.

Shortly after the Virginia Quakers arrived in Maryland, King Charles' worst fear became real. He was arrested by the English Puritans and then executed.

Parliament had known of his America-refuge scheme and was determined to stamp out any resistance there, as both the Virginia and Maryland colonies were sworn loyal to the Stuart kings and had nothing to do with the English Parliament. Parliament decided to forestall the possibility that King Charles I's son (also named Charles), who had escaped execution, might hole up in those colonies and then retake the throne of England.

They gathered a military force of ships and troops and placed it under the command of Richard Bennett. He sailed first to Jamestown and convinced the colonists to swear allegiance to Parliament. He then repeated the process in Maryland. As a result, Bennett was named the new colonial governor of Virginia. Maryland was also given a Puritan governor and the colony eventually taken from the Calvert family in 1688, under William and Mary.

Bennett governed with a fair and gentle hand. That served him well as the Puritan lord protector of Britain, Oliver Cromwell, died of malaria in 1658. With his death, Puritan fortunes in Britain began to wane. By 1660, Charles II was put on the throne of England. Richard Bennett was told to yield the governorship of Virginia back to the previous royal governor, Lord Berkeley. Bennett did so graciously and lived happily with his family in Maryland. Regarding the Maryland colony itself, it was given back to the Calvert family in 1713 under the stipulation that the then-current fourth Lord Baltimore, Benedict, convert to the Church of England, which he did.

I've told this story again because of the clear lesson it presents to any who struggle for power and engage in religious dominance of others. You never know when the situation will change and you'll be on the bottom. With that kind of awareness, America moved more toward tolerance for all in religious matters.

Now for the other colonies. Back in Virginia and other Southern colonies such as the Carolinas and Georgia, a methodical approach to religious practice was proposed by two Church of England clergy—John and Charles Wesley. These became Methodist societies within the Church of England. I attended the first Anglican parish of the Wesleys at St. Simon's Island, Georgia, when I was there in naval service.

All this information sets the stage to address the effect the American Revolution had on religious activities in the colonies. At the beginning, you had these separate colonies with various forms of religious practice. In the so-called middle colonies (New York, Pennsylvania, New Jersey, and Delaware), there was no established religion, per se. In areas under the control of the

American rebels, the Church of England was disestablished—that is, in Virginia, Maryland, North Carolina, South Carolina, and Georgia—in the sense that state funds were no longer provided to Church of England parishes. A lot of Connecticut was still loyal to the English king, so nothing much changed there. Rhode Island was already sort of independent of state religion because of its liberal founding. Massachusetts had no formal ties to the Church of England. New Hampshire never had any formal establishment, but encouraged local areas to provide for the support of clergymen.

All Church of England clergy had taken a personal oath of allegiance to the English king, but quite a few were sympathetic to the colonial cause and ignored their oath. Many parishes were vacant but others continued regardless of the issue of establishment, by renting pews to affluent families and eventually becoming self-supporting by donations.

After the war, several priests managed to become consecrated as bishops. The first was Samuel Seabury. There was a surviving though non-established Episcopal Church in Scotland, still loyal to the Stuarts after the German Prince George had become king of England. Samuel Seabury approached them and they agreed to consecrate him bishop on the condition that he use the Scottish ritual for the Eucharist back in America instead of the one in the English prayer book. That consecration took place in 1784.

Why would they do that? Remember the story in Chapter 4 of the American Continental Congress, in 1782, offering the Stuart heir, bonnie Prince Charlie, the kingship of America? That offer was made because of all the residual loyalty to the Stuarts still present in America among the large numbers of people of Scots descent. Even though bonnie Prince Charlie declined, there were other Stuart heirs alive.

When the English government heard about this, they freaked out. What if America became the home of a Stuart monarchy and that monarchy eventually overthrew the new German line of English kings?

To block this possibility, the English Archbishop of Canterbury agreed to consecrate a second American as bishop—William White of Philadelphia. This took place in 1787.

It is ironic that during the American Revolution Samuel Seabury was a loyalist to the English crown, serving in New York as the chaplain of the King's American regiment. William White, however, was an American patriot, serving as the chaplain to the Continental Congress from 1777 to 1789, at which time, the Protestant Episcopal Church in the US was founded.

Even so, without financial support from the state, there was only slow recovery of the new American Episcopal Church. Most Americans were attracted to what had previously existed as Methodist societies within the Church of England. These people formed their own independent Methodist church, which experienced explosive growth. In many cases, they used former church buildings abandoned by the Church of England. A former Episcopal parish of mine in Howard County, Maryland, was refurbished in the 90s and once again became an Episcopal church.

What about the other colonies? The Congregationalist Church became the established church of Massachusetts and Connecticut. Theoretically, Maryland kept a relationship with the successor to the Church of England in America, the Episcopal Church, until 1970 when the Episcopal Church asked that relationship be severed by a bill in the Maryland legislature. The governor at the time, Marvin Mandell, who was Jewish, was a bit taken back when he learned he was, theoretically, the head of the Episcopal Church in Maryland.

Incidentally, the Episcopal Church in Washington, DC, was not covered by this formal break of relationship. When the federal District of Columbia was carved out of the state of Maryland, all the Episcopal churches in that area were continued to be covered and governed by the Maryland Vestry Act of 1798 until, by a separate act of Congress, that provision was eliminated.[36]

All in all, however, in the new Constitution, the federal government originally left religion as an independent matter for the states.

Thus, the parts of the US Constitution that deal with religion are mainly focused on not creating any federal financial support or preference to either a national church or some particular church group in one in the states. At the same time, the Constitution provided religious liberty protection for some specific groups that had previously been discriminated against in particular colonies. For example, Connecticut had restrictive, discriminatory portions of its state constitution regarding Jews and Catholics that were nullified by the bill of rights.

Otherwise, until the 1940 Supreme Court decision previously cited, a state was perfectly entitled to pay support to a particular religious body. Connecticut did not disestablish the Congregational church until 1818. Massachusetts was the last state to disestablish, doing so with the Congregational church in 1833. Disestablishment originally meant only that a state ceased paying support to a particular denomination.

There is a common belief that the founders of the republic (specifically Madison and Jefferson) were anti-religion. This is not true. Their major focus was to give everybody freedom of conscience and not make trouble between themselves and particular believer communities. I know this to be true not only from family stories but also having gone to the University of

Virginia, known otherwise as "Mr. Jefferson's university," where such history was often discussed.

The picture I have painted in this chapter starts out dark, with intense antagonism between various religious groups. You might say a major motivation for people to come here was freedom of religion for themselves, but decidedly not for others.

This changed. As more and more people arrived, of all varieties of religious belief (and non-belief) a sort of preference emerged for a tolerant form of religion. In more and more of the colonies, no particular religious group was favored. This developed into a common tolerance of other religious groups (although anti-Semitic and anti-Catholic biases were slow to die).

People were becoming assimilated into a unique American way of looking at religion. This was not just blending behavior but also the fruit of hard experiences that when you discriminate against another group today, you may later find yourself to be the victim of that group. On a practical level, better not to judge—look at the world in gray terms, rather than just black and white—just as in racism.

Now, for a final comment to close off this chapter. It is my opinion, backed up by material presented in this book, that the entire relationship between many of the state governments and their religious communities have become severely distorted. As an example, I reference the recent behavior by both the governor of California as well as local health agencies during the recent pandemic.

It was asserted that, in the interest of public health and safety, in-person church services were forbidden. Such services were deemed non-essential and closed, unlike gambling casinos, liquor stores, and marijuana outlets.

The laws on the books of that state were very clear on this matter. In the face of an immediate, serious threat to public safety, the agencies of government are allowed to override the first amendment (the Bill of Rights) of the US Constitution, which clearly states "Congress shall make no law respecting an establishment of religion, or prohibiting the free exercise thereof." The California State Constitution follows this up with similar language.

The accepted commentary on the law addresses common-sense limits to this provision. Interference in the practice of religion is justified only in the face of an immediate, serious threat to the public health and safety, and shall be for a limited duration and consist of only the least disruptive measures needed to address the threat. These matters are addressed at length in California constitutional law: the religion clauses.

In the first application, the referenced paper[37] notes that the federal Constitution's religion clauses were not applied to the states until 1940. Cantwell v. Connecticut, drawing upon the due process aspect of the Fourteenth Amendment, established the precedent for the applicability of the federal freedom of religion clause although it reserves the ultimate right of the state to give preference of its own constitution against that of the federal Constitution. Later on in the article, however, is a large section regarding California constitution-specific law. On page 735 it reads, "The various provisions in California's constitution relating to church-state relations must be read together to create a comprehensive regulatory scheme: free exercise and enjoyment of religion without discrimination or preference are guaranteed..."

People might ask, what is your concern? Virtual services are being broadcast. In the minds of many, religious rites are just a different form of entertainment—words conveying a rationalized teaching or repeating an ancient ritual. This is not true for all. There are many sacramentally oriented Christians. For those people a spiritual happening occurs when there is an in-person gathering. For them, such a thing also occurs in certain types of in-person religious activities.

Some such things are also part of religious activities involving comfort to the ill and dying or saying goodbye to a deceased loved one.

For such people that's why they have churches and religious gatherings. From this perspective, human in-person connecting with the divine and each other is an essential human need, especially during the hard challenges of life. It gives you strength and hope.

Whether only some believe this is not critical. Such a perspective should be respected. To put it simply, a person who does not share the spiritual perspective of others should not decide the rules governing such behavior. That role should be reserved for responsible religious leaders of the people of concern.

There are several religious groups I know of that went underground rather than cease in-person religious gatherings. I know of no one involved in such groups who contracted COVID-19 from such activities, although that may have happened without my awareness.

For many, it is an abomination for a secular official who does not share their religious perspective to forbid them to exercise what, to them, are critical functions of ministering to the spiritual needy, the sick, the shut-in, the dying, and burying the dead. For some such people these needs are as essential as food, shelter, medicine, and medical care, and common-sense adjustments of such religious practices should be left to the particular religious community.

There are a wide variety of ways to accommodate public health concerns for each such community. Such adjustments that fall short of a total ban do involve a calculation and a certain acceptance of risk. The risk assessment must take into consideration the heath of others who do not share the same perspective. As an extreme solution, if such a community were to isolate itself during the time at risk, they should be allowed to follow any set of rules they wish. Otherwise, revise the Constitutional rights to religious liberty.

The necessity for taking serious but calculated risks under certain circumstances has been the glory of the American people. That's how we got to be who we are. What was the risk involved in sailing across the ocean in the early 1600s to a land that offered unknown risks to survival, populated by people who were different, and sometimes hostile? What was the risk to fight a war of revolution, to risk "our lives, our fortunes and our sacred honor" as all the signers of the Declaration of Independence pledged? Why risk one's life in military service? Why take such risks? Freedom to live without the oppression of others makes it worthwhile.

Living under a nanny state is not living. Who is being served by this? The person being restrained or the one who oppresses? Many may not agree, but reasoned disagreement ought to be honored.

CHAPTER 6

WHAT HAPPENED TO ALL THE NATIVE AMERICANS?

Noteworthy takeaways:

- For a variety of reasons, the US census either included no Native Americans in its count from 1790 to 1840, afterwards gave spotty coverage to such people who were living among the general population, no coverage to those living on a reservation (1860–1890), and, after 1900, provided coverage to people living on reservations or those who were living among the general population who knew their ethnicity and who chose to assert it.

- With such systemic undercounting, it is likely that significant numbers of the current US population have a Native American element to their ethnicity of which they are unaware.

- The use by the federal government of treaties with many Native American nations resulted in a population split within those groups, where some chose assimilation and US citizenship, and others were moved to new lands in the West to be under Native American sovereignty. Such treaties were racist and manipulative. There was a continuing history of treaty violation by the US, with major adverse effects on the Native American population.

When a person surveys our country and its current makeup of ethnicities the percentage of indigenous people in the US is estimated at about 1.6 percent of the total population. An important question to be asked is, what happened to make this number so small, and why? Was what happened a good thing or a bad one?

The answer is somewhat complicated.

According to the US Census Bureau,[38] "Prior to 1900, few Indians [sic] are included in the decennial federal census. Indians are not identified in the 1790–1840 censuses. In 1860, Indians living in the general population are identified for the first time . . . Beginning with the 1900 census, Indians are enumerated on reservations as well as in the general population."

So a quick answer is that in many cases, they didn't just vanish, they assimilated. Until 1840 there is no counting of them— at all. As a result, many people in the US with indigenous roots remain unaware of their ancestry. People who were assimilated forgot or chose not to mention it. It is in this time frame, though, that much assimilation took place.

I'll use my own Choctaw roots as an example.

Once the Choctaw were a numerous people. The Choctaw nation was a large, self-governing sovereign entity within the geographic bounds of America. As more and more Europeans came to these shores, there was great competition for land. There was forceful oppression that eroded the land area controlled by the Choctaw nation.

A turning point in this competition came in 1830 when representatives of the Choctaw nation met with representatives of the US government from Washington and negotiated the Treaty of Dancing Rabbit Creek. Excerpts from the treaty are provided in Appendix C. The full treaty with substantial commentary may be found at: https://www.choctaw.org/aboutMBCI/history/treaties1830.html. This is an important reference as the commentary (produced from written daily reports of the deliberations and discussions) documents the full background of the coercion and intimidation applied to induce the Choctaw to sign the treaty, including the threat that the US Army would go to war with the Choctaw if the treaty was not signed.

The major result of the treaty is simple. There was much strife because of competing perspectives on sovereignty. A settler thought he "bought" or was "granted" title to a piece of land by the US or state government when the US did not, strictly speaking, own the land they were giving title to. In short, they were usurping land owned by the Choctaw nation.

Why was this treaty solution proposed and adopted? In a whitewash, the preamble to the treaty states: "**WHEREAS** the General Assembly of the State of Mississippi has extended the laws of said State to persons and property within the chartered limits of the same, and the President of the United States has said that he cannot protect the Choctaw people from the operation of these laws..."

In the treaty, the Choctaw agreed to convey all the Choctaw lands (which encompassed a significant portion of what is now the state of Mississippi) to the federal government with some important exceptions. Figure 3 shows a map of the ceded Choctaw lands superimposed on what then was the future and now is the current state of Mississippi.

Figure 3: Land Ceded by the Choctaw by the Treaty of Running Rabbit Creek[39]

It is noteworthy that the Choctaws had already ceded substantial areas of land in this region to the federal government. If those cessions were to be added to Figure 3, Choctaw lands would cover all of what is now the state of Mississippi plus a good chunk of Arkansas to the east.

What were some of those exceptions listed in the treaty? A person got to choose which sovereignty they would live under. A Choctaw person could choose to remain in the area and become a US citizen. If they so chose, each such person would be given a clear title to a substantial-sized piece of land (hundreds of acres). After occupying that land for five years, the title would permanently pass into that person's ownership.

Instead, they could choose to remain under Choctaw nation sovereignty by being resettled on a new area of land in the West. I am told the very word, Oklahoma, loosely translated from the Choctaw means "nation of the Choctaw." Some chose to assimilate, some did not. Ten thousand Choctaw chose to move West. This is what is called by many as the Trail of Tears.

Even though that Western land (occupying most of what is now the state of Oklahoma) was to be under the sovereign rule of the Choctaw, the terms of the treaty were fulfilled by the US government. A person can read the terms for themselves and see what is unjust and never or only partially honored.

Why was this allowed to happen? The simple answer is greed, elitism, and racism. There was an adverse reaction among some influential members of the American elite regarding the rights granted to the common people by the new Constitution. President Andrew Jackson seems totally contemptuous of the Native Americans.

In addition, note from Figure 3 where the ceded lands are located. There are the very lands that were taken over by greedy, predatory businesspeople once Eli Whitney's invention of the cotton gin made it feasible to grow and harvest large quantities of high-quality cotton anywhere instead of just the coasts. Previously, only long-staple cotton was economically viable to process by hand and that version would only grow in the lands along the coast. Once short-staple cotton could be economically processed using the cotton gin, the cotton business took off and there was increasing demand for slave labor.

These developments fueled the explosive growth of inland cotton plantations (especially in Mississippi), manned entirely by Black slave labor that was to prove so crucial in provoking the Civil War. Mississippi was at the center of the later rebellion. One might wonder, if there had ever been a curb on these predatory people, we might never have had a Civil War. For without those plantations, slavery was already starting to pass from the national scene.

In this context racism can be viewed as a useful tool to disguise the evil behavior of greedy people to oppress vulnerable people (both Black and Native American). It seemed that the gains of the American revolution were being eroded.

Such feelings seemed to be: We needed all those non-elite people to provide the army to defeat Britain, but who needs them now? In the spirit of this reaction, the new Congress passed the Naturalization Act of 1790.[40] The Act set rules for granting of United States citizenship by naturalization. It limited naturalization to "free white persons(s) ... of good character," although some non-white groups were recognized as citizens at the state level.

On the face of it, then, the 1830 treaty might be thought to be in conflict with the 1790 naturalization law, although it could be argued that the 1830 treaty dealt only with people who were already here in America, while the 1790 act dealt with new arrivals. Many Native Americans still became US citizens, often having to deal with discriminatory attitudes against them by new white settlers, although there are notable examples of acceptance.

A discriminatory, racist attitude toward non-whites was a common perspective among the English elite, from whom many of the American elites were descended. Is it any wonder that such attitudes were often held also by common people emigrating from England? These attitudes persisted for a long time.

Indeed, in 1937, Winston Churchill, who was the child of a high-borne English aristocrat and an American mother (Jennie Jerome of Philadelphia) told the Palestine Royal Commission: "I do not admit for instance, that a great wrong has been done to the Native Americans of the United States Red Indians of America or the Indigenous Australians. I do not admit that a wrong has been done to these people by the fact that a stronger race, a higher-grade race, a more worldly wise race to put it that way, has come in and taken their place."[41]

This leads me to the opinion that for a significant number of wanna-be elitist Demagogues, the treaty was only a means to an end—pushing the Native American population off the scene to accommodate their predatory self-interests. This was done by influencing a racist president and intimidating the existing government structure by using commonly held populist sentiment.

Thus, in 1830 the Choctaw people were split into two groups. One assimilated into the broader US population. The other group remained identifiably Choctaw and attempted to maintain their traditional lifestyle and government in their new homeland.

This treaty became the model for the other of the remaining "Five Civilized Tribes,"[42] although the Creek tribes were dealt with first, by military force. In my opinion, those treaties were constantly violated by a US government that was not dealing in good faith. This was accomplished by exploiting common self-serving racist sentiments and a massively racist American president, and is a great injustice.

My conclusion? A significant number of people with roots in the Southeastern US have a Native American component to their ancestry, which is not included in the 1.6 percent figure.

I know this happened because my dad's brother, who lived alongside us growing up, married a woman from Charlotte, North Carolina, who was half Cherokee. Her mother, who was full Cherokee, lived with the family. Nobody in town knew about it (or cared). She was one of the so-called assimilated. (I use the term so-called, because my aunt clearly knew of her own ethnicity.)

Such assimilation was less pronounced when it came to Blacks. A major hindrance was dark skin color. In the town I grew up in, nobody was bothered by little brown-skinned children running around, living in the white part of town, and going to white schools. It's not that some assimilation didn't happen. It just meant there was no assimilation until the skin color of the children "lightened up" enough. When that happened, though, those children were considered white and nobody in the family thought much about it.

There is also another factor—people leaving the reservation. In 1830 the bounds of the new Choctaw nation lands in the West encompassed most of what is now the state of Oklahoma. Nowadays, according to the Choctaw nation's website, "The Choctaw Nation of Oklahoma is a federally recognized tribe whose service territory covers approximately 11,000 square miles in southeastern Oklahoma."[43] Although 10,000 were reported to have moved to the new lands in 1830, the Choctaw nation of Oklahoma website notes that, "The Nation is comprised of nearly 200,000 members worldwide, and it is the third largest tribe in the United States," which is only a tiny fraction of the current US population.

This example covers only a part of the total reservation population of the US and does not include some other Choctaw reservation locations in the US, in particular in Mississippi. A 2010 accounting[44] of the total population of all Native American reservations is about 1.04 million.

It is clear that the population of enumerated Native Americans in the US does not reflect what their once substantial population sizes were unless adverse effects of violence, disease, hunger, etc. were indeed draconian.

I think the answer is that, in addition to the effects of violence, disease, hunger, etc. there is a triad of people in the US with Native American roots. That triad is a relatively small number of people with clear knowledge of their ethnicity who are living on reservations, a small number of those who are assimilated into the greater population and are ethnically aware, and a very large group of people who are unaware due to the massive non-counting and undercounting of people with Native American ethnicity in the US over the years.

CHAPTER 7

Racism—As Defined by Skin Color

Noteworthy takeaways:

- There is a common idea that the concept of race is scientifically tenable. Instead, all the science points to all people, worldwide, being the same.
- This race concept also asserts that not only is the concept of race scientifically tenable, but it can be defined by skin color. This is incorrect. Skin color is a breeding difference between people determined solely by what latitude your forebears dwelled at for a long time.
- The first federal census of 1790 unwittingly provided a court-acceptable proof of a person's race and thus enabled the practical prosecution of existing (but previously unenforceable) laws against race mixing. After this, no white male would risk marrying a non-white woman, no matter what the size of her dowry, and subject himself to potential trial and punishment.
- The US census has now become a major perpetrator of racism by continuing to classify each American documented by that census in racial terms, unless the person opts out of that scheme.

- Application of the doctrine of "separate but equal," promulgated in 1896 by the US Supreme Court in Plessy v. Ferguson was a powerful incentive for promoting racism in specifying different facilities for people according to skin color. If forced a gray world to be divided into a polarized black-and-white one.
- Other countries, such as Brazil, also practiced slavery but seem to have overcome its effects by the natural function of race mixing.
- A significant number of white Americans are ethnically mixed; the same holds true for most Black Americans.

This chapter will focus on and summarize evidence to dismiss as being unscientific the concept of race—that humans are genetically different from each other and this difference can be measured and determined by skin color. I do this because of the centrality of the two concepts of race and skin color that resulted, in my opinion, in the greatest single failure (so far) of the American experiment in self-government—slavery and the racism that defended it and sustained it.

Understand, I'm not attempting to convince you of the truth of the preceding statement in a single chapter but rather summarize the general scientific consensus on the matter and point you to definitive material that you can use to explore the matter further.

Let us begin. During the mid-twentieth century, after the Nazi holocaust against Jews and successes in the civil rights movement in the United States, there was great hope among many that the dubious concept of race had finally met its end. I say "dubious" because even Hitler's Nazi thugs could not, for the life of them, come up with a workable definition of race.

Even so, it seems the concept of race is being given new life. This is especially true among scientists, who should know better. There is a lot of well-funded research going on that seeks to identify particular factors in certain races.

In other words, if you are Black, that "fact" should make you careful about your supposed increased vulnerability to diabetes, for example. When you take a blood test, some of the explanations about the "normal" range of results contain race-specific comments. If you are Black, some of your test numbers have a different meaning than if you are non-Black.

What's going on here? Is this really true? Are we different by race? If so, how do we know what race we belong to? What about people who are multiracial or who appear to be of one race, but are supposedly the offspring of several races?

When you go searching for a definition of race, you are falling down a deep hole. You can't find a reliable definition. It has become popular for people to trace their racial heritage with DNA testing. Companies advertise they can tell you such things with those tests. Those assertions are demonstrably false,[45] but are made to make money from the concept of race. Such comparisons depend on comparing your DNA to that of a sample they have of the noted group. Sometimes that sample group has only a few members and the racial categories depend on knowing what race they came from? Often, they assume the geographic location the samples came from define race.

The British science journalist Angela Saini addresses this topic of the validity of race definition clearly and succinctly in her recent book *Superior: The Return of Race Science*.[46] She writes about the anthropologist Duana Fullwiley who, in 2003, was at the Harvard School of Public Health and spent six months watching and questioning medical researchers in laboratories in California who were addressing the premise that different races suffer from health problems at different rates and can respond differently to treatment.

In the ensuing sixteen years, Saini documents from her interviews that scientists have still not found any meaningful biological definition of race. In spite of this, many scientists and doctors continue to use race as if it's a meaningful biological category. They conflate geography with skin color although there is great diversity in the skin color (and other so-called racial descriptors) of many people in a given locale. The real culprit may be a combination of diet, economic status, health care, and common social practices.

Finally, in the political domain, there's personal advantage to be gained from racism. You can increase your chances of getting into the college of your choice depending on your racial category. There was great controversy over Senator Elizabeth Warren's self-identification to be of Native American ancestry in some early applications for preferential affirmative action treatment in her career. Why was this so?

In the past, the American republic functioned under a set of racist perspectives, and wrote legal contracts with leaders of such groups to gain their assistance in controlling competitors for land and resources who were more numerous, at the time, than white settlers. It was the responsibility of those leaders to keep their people literally "on the reservation" or be punished, for breaking the treaty.

Is this also the perspective that led to affirmative action programs? I view such programs as detrimental to progress in overcoming racism in our society. Why do I say this? Because such programs keep alive the illusion that people are innately different—some superior to others simply because of the color of their skin.

I remember, years ago, when a useful way for people to attack a person of color was a tactic called "kill 'em with kindness." Racists took Black persons who clearly were not qualified or adapted for a particular job and openly promoted them so that, once they were on the job and failed, the racists could say, "See, we tried."

This kind of thing boomerangs against well-qualified capable Blacks who have to carry the stigma of "affirmative action" on their backs. I worked at Lockheed in Sunnyvale, California, starting in 1980. There was an especially great tradition in that company that you didn't need an engineering degree as long as you could do the work.

I took advantage of that in helping promote people (especially women) who were massively talented but didn't have standard engineering credentials. I brought them into my part of the company and told them what they were going to be doing, job-wise. Of course they got nervous but I calmed their fears by saying, "Don't worry. Just trust me. If you get in trouble, I'll back you up." I never had to back up any of the people with whom I tried this. Several turned out to be some of the finest engineers in the company.

In other parts of my career, I had the opposite problem. I knew some truly exceptional people who were ambitious, but were bull-headed about what they thought they had to do. One young woman was one the finest managers I ever knew. She wanted to become a program manager and was convinced she needed a master's degree in computer science to achieve that goal.

The head of human relations (HR) came to me and dumped the problem in my lap. She told me how committed the company was to affirmative action and this young woman had applied to the local university for admission to their graduate program and was turned down. The HR director asked me to get in touch with the university and try and fix things.

I agreed to see what I could do. I talked to the dean and got him to trust me and talk straight. He said, "She has neither the preparation nor the aptitude to be successful as a computer scientist. I told her this and she pressed me on the matter. I told her I could offer her admission, instead, to get a master's degree in computing technology." I immediately saw the problem.

To satisfy its affirmative action goals, the university had come up with a bullshit degree. The student memorized a bunch of data about what was currently available in computing technology and the relevant pluses and minuses of using a particular piece of technology in a certain design situation. It's a bullshit degree because whatever you learn will quickly become worthless as the technology state of the art was advancing so rapidly. Any such degree would become obsolete in value within two or three years, and you would be left with a worthless piece of paper.

I thanked the dean for his candor and said I would work the problem another way. I met with the young woman and told her my opinion about the other degree she was offered. I also asked her to trust me. I asked her why she thought that a degree in computer science was a necessary pre-requisite for her to become a program manager of computing projects? I told her it was my opinion that she had superb talents in management and I would recommend to our superiors that she be put on the fast track for program manager jobs that were coming down the pike. I said, "Just trust me in this for a little while."

She agreed. She became a program manager superstar for the company.

That was an easy one. It is much harder to work with someone who has already gotten one of these bullshit degrees, but does not have the natural aptitude for the work.

The crux of the problem is stereotypical assumptions about the potential for improving human performance. The big assumption is that a person's race has a dominant influence on their potential. Here is what I have learned about human "improvability."

Many years ago, when just beginning a career in naval operations research, I was handed a document called "The U-Boat Logs." It exploited a massive treasure trove of captured German U-boat submarine logs from World War II. By vessel, there was a tremendous difference in effectiveness.

The study concluded that the driving factor in effectiveness lay in the aptitude of the members of each crew, especially the U-boat commander. It derived "measures of effectiveness" with which to grade the submarine and its commander—what characteristics correlated with high performance.

The study then used these measures of effectiveness to predict each submarine's performance, over the time it was in service.

It then presented an amazing set of conclusions. 90 percent of the target kills were produced by 10 percent of the submarines. It went further. If you looked at the effects of training, if a crew turned out to be exceptional in aptitude, it reached a high level of performance after a limited amount of training and stayed there. For the rest, a continued program of training did improve performance slightly each time but, no matter how much training they were given, their performance never got anywhere close to that of the superstars.

If you were looking for performance, the way to achieve it was to select by aptitude followed by targeted training. Again and again, this seemed to be a critical principle in achieving great results. Figure out the metrics of aptitude and then provide specialized training to empower high aptitude persons to reach their potential.

The total focus of my organization was summed up in that example. Our charter was to assist the navy in gaining the maximum in mission effectiveness from the people and facilities it had been provided.

The organization was also built around the stated principle. Figure out what traits correlate with success in doing our work and then scout for high-potential people who possess those traits. After a limited amount of training, each such person was then put to work.

The results were spectacular.

This approach is the opposite of what we are doing in our current educational system. In that system, we make an attempt at selecting likely future high performers, but we have fallen under the delusion that, with less promising students, we can train them out of their "deficiency."

This is made worse by assuming deficiency is related to race. "White men can't jump" (as is sometimes said in basketball circles) may not be an intrinsic factor, but a deficit imposed on a particular group because of a prejudicial culture.

As a result, we have built an educational system with a goal of remedying the deficit by education.

This has given us a problem of national scope. Triggered by pressure for affirmative action compliance (pushed by government bureaucrats), universities all over the country started filling out their rosters with a myriad of worthless courses. The result is heartbreaking. You end up with a young person who wants so much to get ahead, but is being exploited.

A friend of mine was in a bit of financial trouble. He worked with his hands and told me about his son who was eager to avoid falling into his dad's situation. The son had gotten a bachelor's degree and had been accepted into a master's program at a small college. The degree would be in (if I remember correctly) sports activity support, or something like that. His dad was terrified at the student loans he (or his son) would have to pay off. I asked about the course content and said (with some exaggeration), "That teaches you to be nothing more than a glorified water boy."

This kind of problem has gotten totally out of control. So many young people are in hock to pay off student loan debts. At the same time, so many of them have discovered the hard reality that the degree doesn't guarantee a job—aptitude does.

What a betrayal of our youth! Don't get me wrong. A general type of education that teaches young people basic skills, how to think, and what are successful work habits to develop is desirable. Going beyond this should be driven by the aptitude of the person and sensible work aspirations. You should take a degree if you will bring something back from the effort that will be useful or valuable.

It seems like we have built an educational establishment that is self-aggrandizing. It implies anybody can become qualified to do anything with enough training/education. The less responsive people are to training the more training they need and you give them. Want to become rich? Convince young people they can be anything they want to be if only they get enough training. The less natural aptitude, the more training you give them and the more money you make.

Along these lines, categorizing people by ethnicity as a predictor of success or failure is totally misguided. Humans are incredibly diverse in their skills and can discover and develop their particular skills in a proper work setting.

It is easier, now, than when I went to college. Then, I was a poor kid but highly motivated. None of my siblings had my drive. I felt that if I didn't get free of that little town I grew up in, it would destroy me. I had an "uppity" attitude and a certain inclination to use sarcastic speech. My dad told me, "With your mouth and your attitude, you're going to need a steady job." There was some truth in what he said. What was critical in my situation was the power behind my motivation.

I was lucky. I became a naval officer. The training was excellent. I learned a lot of really healthy, useful principles. First and foremost, the navy always gave me a chance. They had the idea they had invested in me so far and they weren't about to not have their investment pay off. They had simple rules like, "praise in public and reprove in private." They (like Yoda of *Star Wars*) weren't big on trying. Do or not do. Trying is for potty-training young children. In short, my experience with the navy was that they wanted to grow people, to build them up to their potential—not tear them down.

The navy quickly discovered two core capabilities in me that were valuable. One (which is obvious to those who know me) is that I have this incredible stubborn streak in me—I never give up. Why am I like that? As I think of my mother and her sisters, they all had the same trait. The trick is to use it for good and not harm. Learn when it makes sense to back off and don't let pride stand in your way.

A second trait they uncovered was that I was cool under pressure. This is called having a "hysterical personality." No, this does not mean I become hysterical in the derogatory sense people use the phrase. It means "hysteresis" as a concept of physics applied to people. Most people, if you turn up the pressure on them, start behaving erratically. The more pressure, the more erratic the behavior. I'm not like that. You turn up the pressure, I stay calm as a cucumber. Eventually, though, there is a point at which the pressure is too much for me and I come apart, emotionally.

The navy used training (where they would systematically put people like me under increasing pressure) to give us the ability to recognize when that coming-apart point was approaching, and take steps to reduce the pressure.

As a result, in a combat situation, I was cool as could be and continued to perform in a calm, reasoned way when others, under the same circumstances, started performing erratically. Such a characteristic is critical if you are going to put a person in charge of the lives of others. Why could I do this? I was the child of generations of military people on my dad's side. Not everyone in the family had the trait, but quite a few did. It exasperated my father when I was growing up. He would try and control my behavior by criticizing me, shouting and yelling as he did so. I knew he loved me and would not hit me or throw me out of the house, so I just ignored all the yelling and let him rant and rave until he was exhausted.

Later on, I got a regular navy commission right out of college. Even though I signed papers and took the oath in an office, he insisted he be there. There he was with tears rolling down his cheeks. At the end he came up to me and said, "Of all my children, you have been nothing but trouble from the first moment you took a breath. You do everything wrong, but it always comes out right. Don't you know how confusing that is for a father?" I saw my opening. I hugged him and said, "I love you too, daddy." He began bawling!

It's so important to know who you are and be that person.

I've given you these two personal examples of what I learned about lifting up people instead of tearing them down, and how important it is to use the education process to help them in that way.

I say this because I see so much bad management and leadership of people going on in the world. I resumed a singing career after decades of being unable to sing for medical reasons. I needed training. I watched as people in authority wouldn't give me a chance because of stereotypical attitudes toward age or they tried to use public humiliation to manage my development. This is the other side of the coin.

In short, I see a lot of poor, misguided leadership in the Black community—much effort on teaching submissiveness and using shame to control behavior. I also see a lot of good. It's a mixed bag.

The point of all this is, my experience tells me that the adverse effects of human deficiencies can be overcome with proper diagnosis to determine a person's core talents and to motivate people for success in those talent areas instead of failure in areas of little or no aptitude.

Yes, people are different. Not everybody can become a ballerina or a rocket scientist. I think that almost anyone can be led into a fulfilling life through proper evaluation and training. I know there is a parent problem here. We sometimes act like we live in that mythical land of Lake Wobegon where all the women are strong, all the men are good-looking, and all the children are above average. Yes, your child has gifts, but we need to find out what they are and help them act on them.

If we are not truthful, however, the family may start blaming the unjust society that trashed their child. Race and skin color are not correlated with human gifts. We need to make sure that there is fairness of opportunity. Right now, in order to be fair, we allocate educational resources according to race, as self-reported. Thus, Black skin becomes a guarantee of Black racist privilege. Our resources are excessively devoted to Blacks in areas where they have less aptitude than some whites or Asians. This assures that, out of our total investment in teaching resources, we will turn out fewer students of excellence. We invent a myth that past racism caused a deficit in Blacks that can be overcome by more training.

How Does This Relate to Race?

Aptitude is not a matter of race or skin color. Is there anything that can be correlated with those things? If not, why? What about disease?

Simply speaking, there are a lot of possible causes that contribute to a given result, and sorting that out can be a difficult problem. Years of investigation, however, have failed to prove any of the so-called racially related causes of disease are linked to race. Instead, they are more likely linked to variations in local conditions and in-breeding of local groups of people while race is irrelevant. This is due to two reasons.

The first is that (like Adolph Hitler) nobody has a consistent way to measure race genetically. Thus, the definition of who should be put into the race versus non-race categories is totally muddled.

The second is that just because many people with dark skin live in a region with a reported health problem doesn't mean the dark skin is the cause. Not all people living in that area, if it is equatorial, will be more likely to have a dark skin than someone from Finland. The foods that are eaten in that region and other environmental effects, as well as lifestyle and economics and health care, are not the same as those in Finland. Confusion between cause and effect is the culprit.

Even so, among peoples who have lived in a region and intermarried for many centuries, there will be a tendency for certain characteristics to be favored and become prominent, from an evolutionary basis, because they are, in some way, favorable to survival and procreation.

A trivial example of this is within my own family. I was surprised when reading tests first started to be given to students. When I took the test, the results were that I could read at about 3,500 words per minute, with over 80 percent comprehension. Later, the same type of test was given to my younger brother. He, too, exhibited the same talent. The same result was documented for both my children who, without any coaching or even mention of this capability, exhibited the same skill. This same turned out to be true for my brother's oldest child.

If survival and reproductive success depended on being able to speed read, my family would have a natural selection advantage. Skin color, however, was irrelevant. With race being defined by skin color, race also was irrelevant. Somehow this capability was being passed down. What mattered was passing on a physiological trait within a geographic group of related people. Skin color was irrelevant. That is the point—that individual differences exist and persist, but they are not explainable in terms of race categories and skin color.

I'll give you another example of how such differences persist, physically—not just mentally—as in my speed-reading example.

As previously mentioned, I was unaware of my diverse ethnic heritage for most of my life. Once I started becoming aware, I was fascinated. All kinds of pieces started falling into place. As I researched the Choctaw component to my ethnicity, I told a friend about some of my discoveries. She became interested and did a little investigation on her own. She then showed me a photo (Figure 4) she found on the internet of a young Choctaw girl. It was taken in 1905 by Carl Moon, an American photographer who spent several years documenting the Native Americans of the US Southwest.

I freaked out. Except for the age difference, the young girl, named Wildflower, could have been my twin. It is obvious that there can be a persistency of some physical features across generations. The photo was taken in Oklahoma. She is descended from some of the 10,000 or so Choctaw who walked the Trail of Tears to Oklahoma. I would guess she is probably of mixed Scots and Native American descent. It is likely she was born in about 1885 or so, only fifty-two years before me.

We humans all have the same number of genes. Our uniqueness is a matter of what combinations of them and their components we have. That's why such coincidences happen. People commonly say things like, "you've got great grandma's nose" or "your Mom's eyes". Maybe this is why people jump to conclusions about race. You tend to reproduce certain features and characteristics from your forbears—not from your race, but from people you are related to. That's the difference.

Figure 4: Photo of Wildflower, American Southwest, 1905

Now back to skin color. It is associated with living in a particular region for a long time. The health problems peculiar to that region are not caused by skin color but other localized factors.

Skin color is one of many inbred characteristics that human have, like red hair. Red hair became prominent because of in-breeding in an isolated locale. There can be other benefits, more than just cosmetic, to having dark skin color that are more important than hair color. Scientists currently believe that all humans were originally dark skinned. Why might this be so?

Originally, humans are believed to have lived in the equatorial regions of the earth where the sun's rays are the hottest. Dark skin provided protection against the severe sunburn and ultraviolet light damage to the skin that would occur for persons who had a light skin living at those latitudes.

What caused the current variety in skin color? Humans became numerous and, with major climate changes, found themselves moving to higher latitudes. Their bodies adapted to this new situation. Why did the bodies need to adapt? Is it just a matter of sunburn?

There is another factor. Simply put, a person with very dark skin living in northern region would suffer a potentially severe case of vitamin D deficiency. This is no small thing. You get ill, and all kinds of damage happens to your body when it is deprived of adequate levels of vitamin D. This is no fantasy from centuries ago. In recent years, when Black people started going to Sweden to work, they ended up with an epidemic of vitamin D deficiency.

This was because the human body has its own vitamin D factory in the cholesterol layer under the skin. Vitamin D is produced when ultraviolet light passes through the surface of the skin and impinges upon these cells that produce the vitamin. If your skin is very dark, in northern latitudes the sun's rays are filtered through much more of the atmosphere. In addition, there are significant seasonal variations in day/night at those latitudes. This means you got much less sunlight on your skin. Also, because of your dark skin color, less of what hits the skin gets through to the vitamin-producing cells below the surface— so you produced less vitamin D—than if you lived at the equator.

This meant that people with lighter skin were healthier and more likely to live and have babies whose skins were lighter. It's like breeding poodles. You pick a trait and only let dogs with that trait reproduce. Eventually, the controlled breeding produces dogs with similar physical characteristics.

The more time goes by, the more pronounced this effect becomes until the common skin color of most of the people in that region is now compatible with less sun. No more vitamin D deficiency. Skin color is not genetic. Darker-skin people just produce more of the skin color hormone, melanin. Same system for all people—different settings of the melanin production system.

This was demonstrated to the world when a body was discovered of a person who had lived many centuries ago in Britain.[47] He was given the name "Cheddar man" —in reference to the discovery locale near Cheddar, England. The world was shocked to find out he was dark skinned. An ancient Briton was Black? Sure was!

All the above discussion is thoroughly explained by Nina G. Jablonski, an anthropologist and professor at Pennsylvania State University, in her 2014 book, *Living Color*.[48]

Why Does This Confusion About Race Keep Happening?

I can provide several answers to this question. One is the tendency for humans to resort to superstition to explain their world. This is a matter of ignorance, however, and is curable by education—showing people the true causes of the effect versus the superstitious ones. This doesn't work with everyone, unfortunately. I remember from college a fellow student had an elderly aunt who lived in the area and kept asking him to fix her radio. She explained she was having trouble getting some of her favorite stations even though she kept changing the vacuum tubes and, "as everyone knows," each tube was associated with a given station. He was unsuccessful in convincing her that the problem was not in the tubes but the declining sensitivity of an older radio.

A more sinister reason is economic. W. E. B. Du Bois explains this in *Black Reconstruction*.[49] You "invent" an arbitrary category, ascribe fictitious traits to each category of people, and then sort people into A and not A. For his subject, the categories were white and non-white. What defined non-white? Some arbitrary, fallacious set of characteristics, such as "kinky hair," "flat noses," and "enhanced sexual libido." The in-group (whites) then takes economic advantage of the out-group (Blacks).

This problem of how to put people into racial categories was raised by a Virginia law that made it a felony for a white man to marry or even have sex with a non-white female. How to prove this in court? Their solution was to use the race notation of the female person or her forbears, as reported in census records, to prove a crime had been committed and send the offending white male to prison. In this law, "one drop of non-white blood" in one official record with the racial notation Black or other non-white descriptor of the person or her ancestor was sufficient to put the female into the non-white category and condemn her partner of the crime. Incidentally, the last time this law was used to send someone to prison was as recently as 1967—in Virginia.

Using such census data, many subsequent analyses have demonstrated that based on the self-reporting entries in the census, a large number of US white people are racially mixed and it also seem true that many US Black people are racially mixed. They are put into white and non-white race categories solely based on skin color. The 2015 Pew Research Center Report, *Multiracialism in America*,[50] presents an exhaustive analysis of this subject. Incidentally, the Black identity being reported is undercounted by an unknown degree because usually a person would only be identified as Black if an appropriate skin color was apparent to them and the census taker.

Regarding the extent of ethnic mixing among Black Americans, the Harvard historian Henry Louis Gates Jr., on The Root,

quotes geneticist Mark Shriver at Morehouse College as asserting that "fully 58% of African American people possess at least
2.5% European ancestry."[51]

Many American Blacks who have lighter skin think that
comes from ethnic mixing with Native Americans. That does
not seem to be true. *The Journal of Human Genetics* published
a study about this and the results seem overwhelming—few
people who identify as African Americans have any ethnic mixing with Native Americans. Their study[52] reports, "We analyzed
the European genetic contribution to 10 populations of African
descent in the United States (Maywood, Illinois; Detroit; New
York; Philadelphia; Pittsburgh; Baltimore; Charleston, South
Carolina; New Orleans, and Houston) . . . mtDNA haplogoups
analysis shows no evidence of a significant maternal Amerin-
dian contribution to any of the 10 populations."

Separate but Equal

In 1896, the Supreme Court case of Plessy v. Ferguson was critical in US history. It established the doctrine of separate but
equal.

Why is this so important? First, it was based on the fallacy
that race could be defined in a scientifically rigorous way. Lack-
ing such rigor, you could assign people to the white and non-
white categories by arbitrary whim based on the fallacy that
skin color defined belonging to a different type of human, a different race. This was the first non-scientific nail in the coffin of
the concept of equal—a problem of having no reliable definition
of race.

The second nail in the concept of equal is the recognition
that equality is only a theoretical concept; it is not present in

reality. I say this because of my work experience in attempting to use equality in my mathematical work.

Mathematically, separate but equal cannot be achieved. It is a concept, maybe a goal, but not something that realistically can be achieved in law and politics.

The Unintended Effects of Certain Laws

There is another factor that I assert has fueled racism in the United States: laws that are unjust and racist by their very nature and other laws that support the practice of racism.

We start with a key question: Why does racism exist in the United States and not in some other countries? Consider Brazil. Brazil was once deeply involved in slavery as an institution, yet today there has been massive mixing of populations of descendants of former Black slaves, Indigenous people, and European immigrants. Why did this happy mixing and tolerance happen in Brazil and not in the United State?

Assimilation of a variety of peoples of different backgrounds is to be expected as the natural outcome of those peoples interacting on a day-by-day basis. Young people are attracted to each other for a variety of reasons that have nothing to do with ethnicity. Put them together and a mix is what will naturally happen. Mixing happens from people with differing appearance and background joining together as a couple and producing babies.

I assert that such mixing takes place naturally without other forces being at play to hinder such mixing.

The family stories I document in this book present several examples of such intermixing as being a common occurrence in the United States. The research I previously cited shows that most white Americans are ethnically mixed and most Black Americans are also.

Beyond my personal family stories, there are plenty of examples of ethnic mixing in America.

Someone as prominent as Thomas Jefferson and his immediate family provide such an example. Thomas's wife, Martha, was the child of John Wales and his first wife Martha Eppes. Martha Eppes died and John Wales then married a Black woman, Betty Hemings, and had a daughter by her named Sally Hemings. Sally was Martha's half-sister. She lived in the Jefferson household and helped raise Jefferson's daughter after his wife died. She even accompanied Thomas to France when he became US ambassador and served as his social host in that country. Genetic research shows that Sally's offspring were fathered by Thomas Jefferson. The relationship between Thomas and Sally became a political scandal during his presidency.

The founding of a Europeanized America was carried out by capable, ambitious young men. They tended to look to Native Americans for wives, European women being scarce in such unsettled areas. Sam Houston, of Texas fame, was originally from Rockbridge County, Virginia. He became very involved with the Cherokee nation and lived with them for several years. That nation even conferred tribal citizenship on him. He married Tiana Rogers, the daughter of a Scots trader and the sister of a Cherokee chief. Many of the first families of Texas started out with such marriages.

There is a wealth of such examples. What happened? It looks like ethnic mixing was widely practiced and tolerated.

Two things happened. First, early on, Virginia passed a law forbidding marriage between a white man and a non-white woman. Other states quickly copied the law. Such laws were generally ignored. How would you prove the crime in a court of law? Outside the law, making such an assertion was likely to provoke a duel.

Then came the establishment of the United States. There was considerable controversy over how to prevent the states with large numbers of Black slaves from gaining political advantage over non-slave states. There was also concern about other areas of the country with a large Native American population. How would you determine each state's representation? The US census was the solution. Using the entries in it, the solution was to only count three-fifths of the recorded Black slave population and none of the Native American population in determining the number of delegates from each state in the new US Congress.

The three-fifths number became irrelevant with the abolition of slavery, but it is now sometimes used to "prove" that Black lives didn't matter as much as white ones, even as far back as the Constitution—a bogus claim.

Without intention, though, there was another use for the census data—to prove in a court of law the race of a woman as noted in that census. When a prosperous person had a large number of daughters to marry off, no white man would take the risk of marrying a non-white woman, no matter how big the dowry her father offered. A person could go to jail under the previous law. The law was specific. "One drop" of non-white blood in the woman was sufficient to prove the offense—one person noted as non-white in her family tree determined from that census. The fragile young white daughters finally prevailed over the Native American and Black ones in the competition for husbands.

Another thing happened. The presence of a past non-white person in your family tree was hushed up. This is likely to have happened in my own family, where a page of the original, official

US census record that would prove the non-white ethnicity of one of my forbears on my mother's side of the family was damaged. Only that part of the one surviving copy of the record—showing her ethnicity—was missing. The rest of that record was intact. Fortunately, I was able to get the data from another record and prove my true ethnicity.

The significant adverse effects of such a system of classifying people may be understandable by a clear reason to do so—to guard against more populous slave states gaining political advantage in the House of Representatives over the less populous states, but that reason was invalidated by the Fourteenth Amendment. Given what we know now about the non-validity of the entire concept of race, it is intolerable to continue the practice of classifying every US citizen by race in the US census. Doing so only continues to give strength to the fallacy of race. We must stop this racist practice.

One more accident of history helps obscure the reality of mixed-ethnicity marriages being something that happens by nature. In the aftermath of the Civil War, the states of the South were prostrate, economically. There were enormous numbers of former slaves loose in the job market with a severe scarcity of jobs. The solution was to demonize the world—divide it into white and non-white. Before the war, whites and non-whites were in close contact with one another. Demonization of the two groups toward each other would be difficult in the face of day-to-day contact.

The answer was the "separate but equal" decision by the US Supreme Court in 1896. Over time, this created two different groups—a white group of haves and a non-white group of have nots, with preference given to the whites for jobs and pay. This allowed the economic exploitation of the non-whites to the benefit of the whites and allowed powerful business entities to play off one group against the other to keep wages down and profits high. When the whites got too "uppity," you just started hiring some non-whites.

I don't want to put all the blame for the growing separation between groups on whites. There were some unintentional effects of what was going on in the Black religious community in the years following the Civil War. Many more Blacks became involved in church activities. They were eager to show their ability to lift themselves up without white aid. There was also a pressing need for specialized attention to the needs of Black folk, as in learning reading and writing. In many locales before the Civil War, such skills were forbidden to be taught. As a result, even in the ethnically mixed Methodist church, Blacks felt a need to have their own church organization.

This is also true in other differences in religious emphasis between white and Black churches. At the time, white churches were focusing on respectability and religious process—proper social behavior. Blacks, however, had a lively focus of their own that tended to be a part of their own ethnic heritage—a kind of robust spirituality that was burned into the individual's soul by personal experience with the harshness of their lives. The "school of hard knocks" taught a resilient core faith that contributed to helping Blacks survive so many decades of oppression. Even now, many white people (and their religious institutions) don't seem to recognize this difference.

For whatever reasons, regardless of intent, there were forces more than just a separate-but-equal court decision that tended to split Black from whites.

Summary

Put all these things together and you have the horror of the American race situation. White (and non-white) as measures of race have no rigorous definition. In such a polarized world, equality of privilege is impractical even with the best of motives. This results in the creation of a perpetual underclass and enables the dominance and economic exploitation of that underclass for the benefit of those who derive financial benefit from the status quo.

Over-reacting to force a solution creates another problem. Allocating educational opportunity by race flies in the face of the founding principle of "all are equal." You now penalize others on the basis of skin color, justifying such prejudicial behavior as righting historical oppression of Black by whites. On an abstract level this is fallacious.

As the testimony of this book has shown, there never has been a systematic oppression of one group of people by another based on skin color. Oppression there has been, but it is situational. Mixed ethnicity was the general state of things for much of the country's history. A Black/white polarization of the world has been developing.

Which Blacks should be rewarded? Which whites should be penalized? The reality of mixed race shows this to be a contrived view of the world. Instead, we need to focus on the individual, on recognizing their particular talents, and making the best use of those talents. The result would be good for the individual as well as the general good of the country.

The solution is to recognize the falsity of race as a concept and stop playing games with racial sensitivity training when the real solution is to work on our society to make sure that, once again, people of all ethnicities are intermingled. We need to unlearn the lessons of separate but equal. Otherwise, we are but playing a game of white versus non-white in a world that, in reality, is composed of shades of gray. In a polarized world, there are only winners and losers. In a gray world, everybody can win.

There is no credible evidence to support the proposition that humans are genetically different due to skin color. Governing influences on their well-being are the environmental factors relevant to that locale and other culturally (group) defined factors. There is no way to scientifically define what race you belong to just by a DNA test, because you can't define race in any rigorous way. Science should concentrate on investigating environmental or culturally defined factors that influence people's health and well-being, and avoid the fallacy of falling into racist thinking.

Let me be explicit about this. People often come up with varieties of labels to stick on others. All these labels say the same thing in the abstract—you are not like me. This immediately leads to the corollary that we are not equal and the follow-on conclusion that "you are inferior to me," so your misery is the fault of being who you are and nothing can be done to change that.

It is so important that people not buy into this game. A person's life is not to be defined by an invented label that is stuck to you. The worst thing that can happen is for a person to accept the label and the self-defeating behavior that comes from such acceptance.

There is a limitation to this reasoning that should be understood, however. Not everyone can become a rocket scientist or a Nobel laureate or a prima ballerina. We are all the same, but there is tremendous variation in talents and traits between individuals that is not defined by race and can either be tested and rigorously applied or ignored as fallacious.

There is another reason to avoid the previously noted fallacious thinking about race. Science should not, by flawed thinking, give credence to the racists of this world. So much evil has been done (and is being done) in the name of racism. I think much benefit for all will accrue by the extent to which we are successful in relegating the concept of race to the superstition trash heap. This includes removing any use of racist labels in the US census.

CHAPTER 8

RACISM, DEMAGOGUES, AND WEALTH

Noteworthy takeaways:

- At its core, wealth ultimately comes from the earth or the sea. It must be accessed by humans. Depending on the favorability of the climate, a given number of humans can live comfortably off a given area. If there are more resources than people the surplus can be diverted into either a higher standard of living or used to free up a given number of individuals from harvesting and hunting to other service work, such as chief, shaman, musician, etc.

- The number of people who can live on the resource can be increased by technology—a plow, a hoe, a knife—up to more sophisticated technology. As the size of the group continues to grow at some point a limit is reached and the standard of living drops below the allowable. At this point, a subset of the group can go off on their own to find their own resource. Other alternatives are to find other untapped resources but, if necessary, use violence to take away someone else's resources.

- Another thing that can happen is to unequally distribute the available resources. Someone can raise their own standard of living by making other people work for them and live with a lower standard of living. A person (or group) can make this happen through violence, intimidation, or clever manipulation. If this is done, the workforce may just walk away. Slavery is used (in its many manifestations) to prevent this from happening.

- America was different. Because of people's access to the bounty of the sea or that of the yet-unsettled frontier, walking away from oppression was possible. This gave people freedom and, with it, personal independence. Those areas of American with direct access to the bounty of the sea or to the free land available on the frontier was where freedom flourished.

- Great wealth can be generated by a combination of three factors—a great demand for the product produced, adequate natural resources, and a large population of cheap controlled labor, who actually produce the needed product. In America, this combination of conditions existed in two places: the cities and the large plantations. In those places, freedom was hard to establish and maintain.

- On the great plantations, racism and the slavery that followed from it was the chosen tool to ensure the availability of the cheap controlled labor needed to produce great wealth. The fiction was established that the races are different and that one was superior to the other. This justified having the superior rule the inferior. How do you recognize the inferior? By their skin color.

- As the cities grew in size, violence, intimidation, and manipulation were used to provide the necessary amount of cheap, controlled labor. Rule by gangs developed. A gang boss gained control of a locale by demagoguery and used that control, enforced by a bunch of subordinate thugs, to make enormous profits off of mostly illegal activities, such as drugs, gambling, prostitution, and extortion. Each gang had a defined territory within which the boss ruled. Eventually, the great goal of a gang and their boss was to use their profits and control structure to expand into legal activities—to go legit.

- Regional difference between a plantation economy in the South (with its emphasis of agriculture and low tariffs) and exploitation of others in the cities in the Northeast (with an emphasis on manufacturing and high tariffs) set the stage for the Civil War.

- At great cost of lives and treasure, slavery was abolished and the slave-dependent plantation economies were laid low. The agricultural products needed in the rapidly industrializing Northeast were now to be provided by the yeoman farms of the Midwest.

- After the Civil War, the economy of the South was devastated, with a great excess of unemployed labor. Jobs were scarce for white people and the situation was even worse for those who previously were slaves but now just lived in camps and had no way to feed and care for themselves and their family. Land was to have been provided for former slaves from the confiscated estates of the owners of the large costal plantations[53] but this was nullified by President Johnson from Tennessee. A Southern sympathizer, he took office after the assassination of President Lincoln. What jobs there were went to unemployed whites. This situation incentivized the growth of racism.

- Later there was a resurgence of oppression in the South. Much of this was achieved by the development and expansion of sharecropping, where unemployed Black people (former slaves) were allowed to dwell on the plantation land and farm an allocated part of it in exchange for giving a share of the produce to the plantation owner. Also, separate but equal justified spreading racism beyond just the revived plantation economies. It provided the ignorance and demonization of others in a racist way that, in a sense, helped nullify the great gains made by the sacrifices of the Civil War.

- What about the cities? There was now a massive expansion of the American economy underway. The expansion was fueled by large numbers of cheap immigrant labor flooding in to meet the labor demands. That growth in population is documented in Appendix A. American GNP (gross national product, the cost of all goods and services provided) grew from the 1830s onward at a rate of two-and-a-half times that of the other eleven developing countries of the world for which the data exists.[54]

- This provided a fertile ground for what had been a practice of demagogue mob bosses to expand their activities from the world of crime into other more legitimate areas of life. This has been going on for a long while and even accelerated with the expansion of the illegal drug trade. Mob-originated dominance and expansion threatens a massive loss of freedom for all Americans who will not be included as part of the governing elite.

- It seems clear that America has not always been a racist country. For the most part it was an under-populated country of vast extent, with wonderful natural resources, providing people the opportunity to walk away toward opportunity. Ethnic mixing was common, not exceptional.

- What changed was the passing of the frontier and the massive, continual growth of the US economy, giving wealthy, powerful commercial interests an enhanced capability to influence and control the government, and practice capitalism in a laissez-faire (anything goes) manner.
- The cry of "racism" is used in many cases as a tactic to silence opposition to gang-related exploitation in the large cities and cloak the motives and activities of such demagogues. In fact, those who will be most adversely impacted by predatory success of an excessively profit-driven unrestrained capitalism will be the poor and most vulnerable, of which the Black and brown are most numerous. It is they who will be harmed the most by defunding the police. It is the gang bosses and their minions who have the most to gain by such tactics.
- These same forces are now at play in the crisis on the US Southern border (i.e., gangs, drugs, human trafficking).

As I have taken the reader through parts of American history, there are certain topics that I think are noteworthy to mention and still a challenge in our time. This chapter will focus on two big ones—racism and oppression by demagogues. I assert both are all tied up with political power and the distribution of wealth.

In basic economic terms, there are only two sources of wealth—the sea and the land. A person needs a certain minimum of those resources to survive—air to breathe, water to drink, nourishment to keep up one's strength, and (depending on the locale) warmth and shelter from the elements and the sun.

In a primitive time, in a favorable warm climate, one can survive quite well by living off the land. I learned this from survival training in the Okefenokee Swamp in Georgia. The trick was to know the locale—what plants to eat, what snakes are poisonous, etc. With such knowledge it only took a few hours each day to gather berries, find the right roots to eat, what game to catch and eat, and the same for catching and eating fish from the same stream you drank from. It was a veritable Garden of Eden, but it took a little technology to make efficient use of the bounty. Fishhooks, a knife, matches to start a fire, and a parachute to use for shelter and to make an enclosure to smoke and preserve protein (fish, snake) for later consumption.

That being said, there was a limit to the number of people who could subsist off a particular locale. With too many people, you could hunt out or fish out protein sources and run out of particular kinds of vegetables. In another context this would be called overgrazing. Without some of the technology you could still do okay, but the cost would be more time spent searching for and preparing food. You could do away, for example, with fishhooks and, instead, use your knife to make a spear out of a wood branch, and then use the spear to spear a fish in the stream. It just took more time.

So, people are suited to successfully survive in a favorable climate, but there are limits to how many people can be supported by a given area. Technology helps you do that. A knife is critical, but to make a knife you have to gather ore from the ground, process it, and form the resulting metal into a knife. Here, it helps if you have particular persons specialized in processes that people need done—like miner, farmer, cook, hunter, blacksmith, etc.

In simple terms, a given number of square miles will only support a certain number of people. In addition, everyone must do their part or fewer people will be able to be clothed, fed, etc. Every person who does not contribute makes life a little harder for everyone else.

Even so, a person skilled at violence or intimidation can force others to take up his or her share of the burden.

At some point, for a variety of reasons, the area will have become overgrazed. The group must then leave and find a new fresh area. If they don't, they will starve. They may find a good new area, but discover another group is already there. They can continue their search or use violence to take the area from the others. This is the human dilemma. A given area will only support so many people.

Technology can have an important positive effect on how many people can be supported, but it is particularly costly if some do not contribute, but, instead, live off the effort of others.

Finally, this is not a sharply defined matter. There's such a thing as standard of living. The more available labor you have in excess of what is required to meet essential needs, the more people can be excused to do important service kind of work—like being a judge, a tribal leader, a warrior, a musician, a shaman, etc—or to produce luxuries, things people want that are beyond their survival needs.

I wrote the above material to give the reader a basis for what I'm going to say next, which directly impacts the success of a society. If a subset of the group (an elite) figures out they don't have to work at all or is greedy for wealth, but can use violence, intimidation, or manipulation to force others to work in their place, you have introduced oppression into the situation.

Oppress means to push down. You push down the standard of living of others to artificially inflate your own standard of living. You have a large number of oppressed people who are being exploited to meet the needs of a ruling elite.

This is called the problem of wealth redistribution. At some point, the system falls apart if the persons providing the essential roles decide to quit and leave. This is why you have slavery in all its forms—to use violence, intimidation, and manipulation to force other people to do your bidding, to prevent them from quitting or engaging in revolt.

America broke the cycle of such societies. It provided the circumstances for the independent farmer, trapper, or fisherman to meet their essential needs. The ability to not be forced by violence, intimidation, or manipulation to work to support others is called freedom. America showed how it could be done.

There were challenges, however. The cities, in particular, were efficient concentrated sources of power from which the dominant elites can control the populace inside the city. Because of the greed of those at the top, there were not enough rewards to go around. No matter, as long as you controlled the masses.

Let me give you a simple explanation of oppression as practiced in the cities. Many people in cities use intimidation, violence, and manipulation to oppress others. Such a controlling elite are true laissez-faire capitalists. They prey upon others to elevate their own lifestyle and satisfy their cravings for greed and power. How do they do this?

First, they use gangs. Such gangs are individual little countries, by themselves, often defined by ethnicity, with fixed geographic bounds between them and other gangs. A gang boss is the local demagogue and has a group of enforcers to do his bidding. They recruit new members when they are young—getting them involved in the perpetration of illegal acts, including murder, theft, and rape. Once branded, the recruit cannot walk away without the threat of being fingered out to the civil authorities as a perpetrator of illegal acts. This has been the nature of gangs in large cities throughout history. In the past, gangs thrived in exploiting illegal activity within their boundaries—bootleg alcohol, gambling, and prostitution, for example. To this list can be added the trade in illegal drugs. Get people hooked and then squeeze them for every dime.

Such an arrangement is totally hostile to the police. A police force dedicated to gang-busting threatens the world they have built.

This was the original motivation for having police in the first place. In London in the 1800s, the elite had their own protection—either paid individual personal protection or the elite were granted special protection rights, like being allowed to carry a sword. In a world where knives, clubs, and fisticuffs were the usual means of violence, having a sword and knowing how to use it provided great protection. In a world without guns, the person with the longest knife—who knows how to use it—wins!

In 1829 Sir Robert Peal (twice British prime minister) established a force to provide protection to the non-elite. These became named "bobbies" in his honor. They carried a club and could quickly summon backup with their whistle. The idea of such a police force spread around the world.

In principle, nothing has changed. The elite can easily provide for their own protection. It is the non-elite who suffer without effective policing of the cities to hold the gangs at bay. Obviously, the gangs would like nothing better than either abolishing the police force or intimidating it to stop functioning.

From this perspective, the violence in our cities is a perfect example of the threat of demagoguery made manifest. The violence is a response both to oppression as well as a propagandized representation to the people that racism is the cause of their woes—not repression by greedy economic elements in their cities, many of which are of the same ethnicity. In other words, white racism is being used as a boogeyman to deflect attention from a major problem—demagogue and gang-related oppression within the Black community directed at other Blacks.

Because of threat of such demagoguery on a broad scale, the founding fathers rejected the idea of having a pure democracy. Why? As in my city violence example, they were aware of the problem of unscrupulous individuals who could manipulate the masses of people with empty promises in order to gain power and, once power was gained, could use that power to maintain their position.

The unsolvable vulnerability here that made a pure democracy unworkable was the susceptibility of the common people to being manipulated and intimidated and to be unable to critically assess the truth of what they were being told.

This is a problem of ignorance. It has a solution—education. Unfortunately, there were not enough resources available when the country was founded (although Thomas Jefferson wanted to set up such a public education system). Society did not, at that time, feel it could afford mass public education.

The solution of the founding fathers was to have a popular vote, yes, but to have the actual election of leadership put into the hands of educated people who could see past the wiles of the demagogues. This is why we have a republic and an electoral college.

Still, there is a critical reason to have a popular vote. The system comes apart if those who rule become isolated from the situation and needs of the people of the country. You don't need a college education to say ouch! The electoral college is supposed to consist of people who are in touch with the needs and feelings of the people whose will they represent. A popular election is a means by which the population can express their needs and wishes. Without a popular vote, the risk is that frustration and dissatisfaction will grow until it explodes in violence. The popular vote is intended to prevent such an explosion from happening.

Even so, the people of the country need to be vigilant in expressing their needs and in holding accountable those in power who ignore the people's needs. This includes the needs of all the people.

Unfortunately, too many people are trained in the techniques of propaganda—how to lie and be believed. Without such a capability, protection against demagogues would be easy. You just listen to what they promise and then measure their performance against such promises when they get into office.

The defense that prevents this from happening is truth. Propaganda is ineffective if your opponent can counteract your propaganda lies with verifiable truth.

Without a critical, informed populace any evil fool has the chance to gain power by promising people impossible things. Once in power, they proceed to not follow through on their promises. This is why you need a free press for a republic to function. The job of that press is to be the people's watchdog. If, however, evil demagogues ever gain control of that press, lies become unchecked and demagogues are not held accountable. They use selective lying to various groups to gain their selfish support. There is no mechanism to track such manipulation and report it to the people.

There's one more critical development that has changed the scene and people's vulnerability to be controlled—drug addiction. This was a big problem in cities and has now grown to be a problem outside the cities. The technique is simple. You get vulnerable people hooked on drugs so they must have them. If you control the distribution mechanism, you control the people who use the drugs.

Like any mob boss, your control (using the money you gain at such a lucrative enterprise) allows you to maximize the amount of money you can extract from people. You have an army of pushers to milk the community of its money. The people who are addicted become your slaves. Their only purpose in life is to give you a steady stream of wealth that flows from the addiction. This is one reason why many of the big cities are so corrupt and already under the rule of demagogues, and why the threat is expanding more broadly.

OK. So much for the topic of distribution of wealth and how best to manage that.

What happens if a demagogue does gain power? What recourse do the people have? The answer was supposed to be the First Amendment—the right to keep and bear arms. This was not some obscure reference to how you maintain a militia. It was to be the last-ditch defense of the people against oppression—mass armed civil disobedience.

This is still true for mob violence. If the police cannot provide protection the ordinary citizen must be able to protect themselves.

Many Americans with British roots knew their ancient history. Once, Britain was a province of the Roman Empire, conquered in the latter part of the first century AD. Under Roman rule, it was forbidden for common people to be armed. The argument was that Rome would defend them with its legions and having ordinary people running around with weapons, and who knew how to use them, just set the stage for rebellion.

In the latter part of the fourth century AD, the situation changed. There was much conflict in mainland Europe between military heads of legions competing to become emperor, as well as pressure from non-Roman tribes such as the Visigoths. In AD 407, the last of the Roman legions were withdrawn to the continent. They never returned. Outside forces (Saxons, Scots, Picts, and Angles) now saw Roman Britain as a ripe target for plunder. In AD 410, there was a desperate plea sent to the Emperor Honorius for Roman military forces to repel these outside attackers. Honorius' reply was that he had no forces to spare and the Britons needed to look to their own defense.

Things just got worse and worse, although the Britons now tried to replace the Roman presence with their own kings and magistrates.

By the early 500s, according to the British priest, Gildas,[55] the Britons had asked the Saxons for help defending them from the Picts and Scots. By treaty, the Saxons agreed to do so in exchange for food supplies. Once established, however, the Saxons broke the treaty and took over the region of Southern, Western, and Eastern England (Sussex, Wessex, and Essex). Eventually, their rule spread over all of what is now known as England, the domain of the Anglo-Saxon kings. Britons either left their homeland and resettled in what was then still Roman territory in the Northwest part of Europe (known as Brittany) or retreated to the hilly West of England, now known as Wales. Gildas migrated to Brittany and founded a monastery there.

The message was clear to the founding fathers, never put your complete trust in others to protect you. If they fail or are no longer available, you need to have a backup of people with arms and the skills needed to use them. This was the last line of defense against those who would seize power and then take away your liberty.

This was tried once in the American Civil War, for an inappropriate cause. It failed. The reason it failed was not the justness of the cause but the numbers of troops and quality of support of the Union forces compared to those of the Confederacy.

Also, there's a basic problem in the use of violence to achieve a political aim. Once you let go the dogs of war and violence, you have real problems reigning them back in. The violence tends to become uncontrollable and takes on a life of its own, driven by mob psychology.

A great Black leader, Frederick Douglass, after having been a strong proponent of non-violence, eventually was won over to the necessity for violent action.

As a result, after all the outsider troops went home there was a reactive vengeance against Blacks by many white people. This is the danger of using violence, even in the most just of causes. There was plenty of anger to go around. The South was a defeated, occupied country, with an economy in ruins. The adverse consequences were imposed on everyone—Black and white alike—but it was easy for whites to blame and scapegoat Blacks for the misery all suffered. Unfortunately, Blacks had not gained the critical element—land—which would enable them to retain their freedom. To survive, they either submitted to the oppressor or moved to the big cities, when a new type of racial oppression was in play.

This challenge is still with us. The Reverend Dr. Martin Luther King Jr. never gave in to the call for violence. There are many in today's Black community who disagree with that approach, who say it's out of date and left the problem of racism unsolved to just fester again later.

It's my own opinion that the massive gains of the civil rights movement of the 60s would have never succeeded without the goodwill and support of many white folks, whereas a more violent approach would have alienated that necessary support.

My great fear is that, having resorted to violence, history will repeat itself with a savage repression of Blacks by whites, the Blacks having used up much of the sympathy and intrinsic goodwill of the general populace. This would leave behind nothing but anger, which might cause a loss of much of the very impressive progress achieved in civil rights since the 1960s.

Originally in America, ethnic mixing was almost the rule rather than the exception until after the American Revolution. Since then, people have lost awareness of how ethnically mixed most of us are. In reality, we live in a gray world but act, in our minds, as if we lived in a black-and-white world.

Such a binary world is one of sports—zero-sum games where one team wins and the other loses. Such a world has no final winners or losers. Just wait until next year, and the positions could reverse. It is a world of endless strife. Instead, behaving as ethnically mixed people, the world becomes one where win-win solutions are possible. Everybody wins. We reconcile as long-lost members of the same family.

A lot of blame for current racism must be laid at the feet of the US Supreme Court. In 1896, in Plessy v. Ferguson, the court ruled that the equal protections mandated in the Constitution were carried out if Blacks and whites lived in worlds that were "separate but equal." The disastrous consequences were the result of the Supreme Court trying to placate a bunch of racists in the states of the old Confederacy by justifying repressive rules and laws against Blacks, while pretending to honor the "equal protection" clause of the Constitution's Fourteenth Amendment.

It was a disaster. By separating people of different ethnicities into separate communities, you deprived people of the healing, reconciling benefits of Blacks living intermixed with whites. You could learn to hate the other group because you didn't know anyone of that group, personally, and could demonize them as different and, therefore, inferior to whites. This worked because the metric of difference was skin color, which had nothing to do with whether one person was superior or inferior to another. Fear is an important tool available to manipulate and control people. In the case of racism, this is fear of the *other*. This is effectively confronted if you eliminate the ability to demonize others through the use of social and cultural separation.

Skin color was a major factor in enabling the oppression of Blacks. You could now use the census entry about a person in a court of law to enforce racist laws. Before there was a US census, racist laws, although on the books, were almost impossible to prosecute.

The problem such laws ignore or side-step is that there is no tangible, physical world-based thing such as race. There is no scientific evidence of a difference between people (especially as measured by skin color difference) based on race.

There are difference between people such as hair type, nose type, and more, but these are the consequences of breeding. I may be a poodle or a Saint Bernard, but both are just different types of dogs.

There was another factor that re-energized racism in the agriculturally oriented South. The economy was devastated by the destruction of the slavery-oriented plantation system. In addition, the yeoman farms of the Midwest, with the buildup of the railroad system needed there to get produce to market, had taken away the market share of the produce market in the Northeast. The South could not compete. There were massive numbers of former slaves with limited skills and unable to find work.

This situation was turned around, gradually, by the development of sharecropping in the South, where the large number of unemployed (and homeless) former slaves were allowed to live on the owner's land and allocated a part of that land to grow produce. The price of this arrangement was that the sharecropper had to provide a certain percentage of the produce that was grown in exchange. The landowner had all the control and could, in effect, re-institute the former slave labor-based economy under just another name. The farms of the South could now compete with the farms of the Midwest.

As a result, the freedom of the former slaves was gradually eroded and the same argument of racism used to oppress them. Indeed, this was one of the unspoken arguments used to justify the Plessy v. Ferguson "separate but equal" US Supreme Court decision. In effect, it used a racist argument (it is a sin to mix the races) to appease the landowners of the former Confederacy and justify a return to slavery while pretending to honor the Fourteenth Amendment protection of equality.

In this way, the racism status quo returned or got worse. Racism spread to the rest of the country as the demand for super profits (obtained by the exploitation of cheap labor) spread across the rapidly industrializing country.

One choice the former slave had was to choose oppression under sharecropping. The other choice was to leave for the cities of the Northeast (and the industrializing Midwest) to compete with cheap immigrant labor in the demand there for a massive amount of cheap labor. This was also working under oppression.

This is why I say that racism increased in America in the years after the Civil War and, I think, started to peak at the turn of the century.

The culprit in both cases is lack of curbing the immorality of predatory labor practices undertaken in pursuit of increased profits.

The good news, I assert, is that we should be able to solve the race problem with education and increased inter-ethnic social interaction. The education should be to debunk the fallacy that there is a scientific basis for race, and also recognize that we live in a gray world of ethnicity, not a-black-and-white one that, as previously discussed is an us-versus-them world, so there is continued struggle for dominance instead of a win-win situation where no one, according to their skin color, gets to dominate others.

There is another factor that must be addressed—originally well-meaning but ultimately self-defeating laws that are passed to help, but make a person dependent on the state. The trouble is that, once dependent, the person suffers if the public support is removed. They no longer know how to get their needs met in other ways. In the abstract, this is no different than drugs. A person trapped in this system has no choice but to kowtow to their local political bosses.

This is a major factor in the destruction of the nuclear Black family. It produced female heads of large families because the laws, as written, incentivize such behavior. To me, this is nothing more than plantation economics—put people into an economic situation that works to keep them captive and provide them with just enough to satisfy political control of their behavior.

We need to make better use of education to uplift all our young people to identify their unique talents and help them develop them, instead of trying to fit everyone into a rigid, pre-conceived set of slots, which only leads to low self-esteem and poor performance.

Finally, I should mention something else that is important—political indoctrination of young people. If you tell them things when they are young, and keep repeating the message by both your words as well as your behavior, correcting erroneous behavior is difficult.

We see this in religious radicals such as ISIS. Actually, though, this is just another dimension of using education to dispel ignorance. The difference is that beliefs indoctrinated in the young at an early age are difficult to change, even with good education.

On a final note, the use of violence and intimidation and manipulation of others by powerful groups in the service of greed and ego has expanded well beyond the world of city gangs. Other powerful elements of our society have begun to emulate the tactics of the gang boss.

Now is the time to stamp out such practices or give up much of our freedom. In doing this, we should not be misled by shouts of racism being used to silence opposition. Some of those who scream the loudest are simply using the situation and manipulating it to gain more power themselves, and are exploiting the naive and out of touch who know nothing of such a world of violence, intimidation, and manipulation.

Such hollow and manipulative activities need to be undercut by sincere attention on the part of Congress in restraining oppressive labor practices. Focus on eliminating the root cause of oppression, while using the gentlest ways to reduce violence—education and reform. There is a problem with systemic oppression of the labor force by the unrestrained pursuit of excessive profits.

Ironically, holding back on restraining violence (defunding the police) will have the most adverse impact on those least able to defend themselves—in particular, the poor and underprivileged of color. They will suffer the most from a lack of progress.

CHAPTER 9

CONCLUSIONS

Noteworthy takeaways:

- There are many good, unique things that flow out of the American "experiment" in freedom. The American Revolution worked to provide true freedom because the abundance of food from the sea and land available to all on the frontier allowed people to walk away from oppression.

  There is a common idea that the concept of race is scientifically tenable—that people are different. There is absolutely no scientific basis for this. Instead, all the science points to all people, worldwide, being the same. A corollary finding is that skin color is irrelevant in this matter.

- A major conclusion is that a substantial part of our population is ethnically mixed. Together with the previous takeaway this has resulted in us living in a polarized black-and-white world while scientific and historical reality defines a world that is gray. This misconception is a major obstacles to progress in solving our national race problem.

- There are three areas of serious concern and deficiency with regard to the balance of power between the branches of government.

  - First, the safeguards against government takeover by a demagogue are out of date. Progress must be made in ensuring that unbiased information is available to the voters. A set of fair election laws needs to be developed to give the citizenry assurance that their votes will be counted, their voices heard, and illegal voting prevented.

– Second, the practice of judges "rewriting the Constitution" by their rulings must be curtailed and the Constitution updated to address new challenges.

– Third, the practice of a president ruling by executive order and going around Congress is the rule by edict that was practiced as the Roman republic was turned into a dictatorship and that so concerned the founding fathers of the US republic.

• We need to have a solution that will, once again, enable Congress to perform the lawmaker function. The problem is a divided nation, as reflected in a divided Congress.

• The issue of fair wages for American workers must be satisfactorily addressed. Evasions by outsourcing labor to foreign countries and the abuse of illegal immigration must be stopped or the US will become another Venezuela. We need fair immigration reform and not xenophobia.

• The federal government must satisfactorily address the historical injustices inflicted upon Indigenous peoples, especially with respect to broken treaties.

Based on the discussion and information presented in this book, I drew conclusions about what's good about America and what isn't good. I haven't taken particular care in identifying a past problem area where a good solution has never arisen or a previously good solution to an issue is no longer adequate, and why.

There are significant topics of controversy this book has not addressed that are, for the most part, beyond the specific scope of our current Constitution. An example of such an issue is the government taking over responsibility for the care of people, instead of this being the primary responsibility of the nuclear family and private institutions. I avoided addressing such topics in this book because they are issues that have developed within the memory and experience of many of our people, so past personal history of my family is not relevant.

Beyond such out-of-scope topics, though, there are several important broad issues the reader might think about and decide what response they would favor.

The first issue is, assuming the founders' vision was correctly captured and presented by the author, is that vision still valid or has it become fatally flawed?

Second, if the original vision is considered to be no longer workable, what is the alternate vision?

Third, if only a modified (or amplified) version of the original vision is needed, what are those needed changes?

I have no intention of answering these questions. To do so requires great political skills that are not part of my toolbox and, most importantly, assent from the populace to have meaning. To restate my perspective, I consider it my job to adequately present the original vision, to ask informed questions about perceived deficiencies, and render opinions about what parts of the original vision are still valid and what are challenges to that vision that need a compelling public response and agreement.

To start, let's create a list of what's good about America.

1. First and foremost in America's heritage of goodness is the concept that all are created equal. This is unique. In practical terms, it means that everyone is given the opportunity to pursue their dreams, without such opportunity being forbidden to or limited to particular segments of society. There is a corollary, however—accountability. You

may suffer failure, but the consolation is that such a failure was a consequence of your own choice.

You are not punished for the failure of others. This equality was quite a new thing at the time of the founding and emergence of the country and appears to have come as a direct result of Quaker teaching on this subject being widely accepted throughout the populace. In practical terms, this translates into the concept that governments are created to serve the people, not the other way around. There was also a fluidity, an openness to class and even ethnic mixing.

2. Widespread acceptance of such a concept could only have come about because America was a marketplace for competing ideas—especially with regard to religion because of freedom of religion. This was a new thought in the history of governments. Previously, organized religion had tended to be an arm of the government.

3. Great natural resources—especially lots of land—made it possible for most to own land. The great availability of both game and the protein wealth of the sea were also special. No one needed to go hungry. This includes a relatively temperate climate, amenable to agriculture. I consider this lack of land being given to freed slaves as an obstacle that, ultimately, prevented the sacrifices of the Civil War from setting the stage for an elimination of the race problem. Incidentally, this was recognized and provided for by Union Army General William T. Sherman. His Special Field Order No. 15, of January 16, 1865, confiscated 400,000 acres of land from Southern plantation owners to be redistributed in forty-acre segments to former slaves. Unfortunately, he was later overruled by President Johnson.

4. For most of its history America has had a scarcity of labor, of people. From a positive point of view this made the labor of each valuable, but also promoted slavery and other forms of bondage to make up the insufficiency of labor.

5. Because of a plenty of yeoman citizens, most of whom were skilled in the use of firearms for hunting, there was a broad capability for national defense centered around gathering together those people into an army or militia in time of threat. A similar capability existed for a navy, because of the great number of skilled watermen and sailors.

6. There was a lack of oppression. Except in the case of the national curse of slave labor, it was difficult to force people to act against their wills, which is the essence of freedom from oppression which most new emigrants were seeking. This resulted in an independent, self-reliant populace in many parts of the country.

In one area, the United States seems to be especially cursed—racism. From this perspective, some people are considered to be different from other humans in racial terms, as measured by skin color. This book presents ample evidence that there is no scientific validity nor physical reality to such concepts. They exist only in the minds of some people.

Even so, these concepts were found useful in creating an artificial subset of humanity that was inherently inferior to others. This provided an artificial boost to the living standards of others and would be especially helpful in creating and maintaining a privileged ruling elite, whose privilege was built upon the exploited labor of others.

When the American republic was created, major effort was focused on giving people the freedom to make their own choices in life and suffer the personal consequences of bad choices. This was opposite to letting those choices be driven by a ruling elite who might seize power from the people and use it for their own selfish benefit.

The approach taken in developing and defining the new form of government was to carefully examine history for precedent and examples to be considered and used to build in safeguards intended to prevent a recurrence of those mistakes in the new government.

In the face of the preceding (and impressive) elements of goodness, what were the areas where the vision, as implemented in the Constitution, either failed or fell short of the mark?

Table 1 is a summary of the information and discussions of this book regarding major concerns for the new government. It presents a recap of the issues addressed, what solutions were proposed, and the result.

As you go through the list of challenges in the first column, you'll see great emphasis being placed on the threat posed by a demagogue gaining and maintaining power to oppress the common people and take away their liberty. The fear was the new government would be vulnerable to the establishment of a new homemade elite ruling class as bad for the people as the foreign one was.

Table 1: Constitutional Issues and Responses

Challenge	Proposed Solutions	Results
Demagogue gains power by false promises to direct voters	1. King of America	1. Stuart heir declined offer
	2. Government-funded public education	2. Jefferson proposed by not funded
	3. Electoral College	3. Accepted, but not applied as designed
Demagogue seizes power by manipulating information available to voters	4. Free press	4. Modern information control makes vulnerable
Demagogue uses voter fraud to be elected	5. Strict voting laws applied	5. Accepted; successful but laws may be eroded or ignored
Judges can issue precedent-setting rulings	6. Confirm only strict constructionists by Senate	6. Changes in political party—gain control of Senate
		7. Intimidate or manipulate Supreme Court
One branch usurps power	8. Military officers swear allegiance to Constitution	8. Tradition of apolitical military; prosecute infringement
	9. Presidential rule by executive order	9. Amend Constitution
Constitution becomes outdated	10. Amend Constitution	10. Political evasion of process
All created equal (anti-elite)	11. Fourteenth Amendment	11. Overturn Plessy v. Ferguson
Indigenous conflicts	12. Treaty	12. Remedy US treaty violations
Lack of muscle labor	13. Imposed labor	13. Slave labor (compulsory)
		14. Technology
		15. Outsourcing

The founding fathers were fearful about creating a pure democracy. Their reading of history led them to the opinion that all such prior attempts had failed because a demagogue would take advantage of people and trick them into giving away their power.

With so many pro-Stuart elements present in the population of the time, in 1782 a committee was formed and delegated the authority to approach Bonnie Prince Charlie who had attempted to regain the throne of Britain, and offer him the role of king of America. He had failed in his attempt to gain the British throne with a major defeat of Scottish forces at the Battle of Culloden and had retired, in exile, to Rome, with the assistance of—and under the protection of—the Pope.

The mission failed. Prince Charlie turned down the offer citing old age and his feeling he had failed in everything he had attempted and did not have an urge to repeat that history again.

The founders finally settled on the idea of a republic, rather than a pure democracy. They had several specific fears regarding the susceptibility of such a government to seizure of power by a demagogue. Their specific fears were false promises made to an ignorant, and therefore vulnerable, population. Another was the use of violence (as in a military coup) or intimidation to effect such a goal. Another fear was the demagogue would somehow seize power by manipulating the information available to voters. Another fear was voter fraud.

They addressed these fears by providing the following features of the new Constitution as solutions. First and foremost was an electoral college to prevent the election of a demagogue. There would still be a full popular vote by all to provide an input to the electors, who would take all the people's concerns in the election into account. But the electors themselves would, in the extreme, be able to vote their own consciences. This was the way to finally and conclusively eliminate the threat of false promises and manipulation. Unfortunately, at this point in history this solution is only a theoretical one. Were the electors to use the powers they are granted under the Constitution, a hue and cry of "foul" would create a constitutional crisis that would likely be resolved by amending the Constitution to eliminate the Electoral College from that document.

Were their fears exaggerated and unfounded?

Another way they addressed the fear of rule by a demagogue was the idea of separation of power among the three branches of government. This is now a substantial threat to the continuation of representative government, as we have known it. In the face of a divided nation, which results in a divided Congress, in gridlock, the temptation is for the executive branch to rule by edict, using executive orders to bypass Congress. Left unchecked, this practice will totally undermine our system of representative government and lead America down the same path that resulted in the demise of the Roman Republic and subsequent rule by power-mad Caesars.

Even so, we don't have to go back to the time of Caesar for an example. Look to the Nazi takeover of the German Democratic Republic in the 1930s by Hitler and his fascists. Figure 5 presents the timeline of that takeover and how it was achieved.

It took only twenty months to complete from start to finish. Here was a country in political turmoil with the fascists on the right and the communists on the left, vying for power and a paralyzed parliament in a deeply divided nation.

The parliament had a lot of middle of the roaders, but they had been rendered ineffective when faced with the vehement partisanship of the extremists from both sides. Note the use of an invented crisis, a German tradition of anti-Semitism, and the burning of the parliament building (allegedly by the Communists and their atheistic Jewish collaborators) to justify a grant of emergency powers to Chancellor Hitler. That power grant overrode the civil rights safeguards of the German constitution, which was modeled after the US Constitution.

Figure 5: A Modern Manifestation of a Demagogue Taking Control of a Democratic Republic

- General Paul von Hindenburg was highly respected and trusted by the people of Germany. He had served honorably in WWI, coming out of retirement to do so.
- In 1925, he returned to public life to become the second elected president of the German Weimar Republic.
- In November 1933, in the face of national political instability and economic hardship, the German people gave the Nazi party a plurality in the elections, based on Adolph Hitler's promise that, if elected, he would fix things.
- In January 1933, despite private misgivings, General Hindenburg appointed Adolph Hitler Chancellor of Germany (the office of the German prime minister).
- On Monday, February 27, 1933, precisely four weeks after Hitler was sworn into office, the Parliament building of Germany, the Reichstag, was set afire by arson.
- In response, President Hindenburg signed the Reichstag Fire Decrees, which temporarily suspended various civil liberties guaranteed to the German people by their Constitution, which was modeled after that of the United States.
- Hitler blamed the fire on the Communists as part of a coup to seize power. Using his temporary powers, he

expelled all Communist members of the Reichstag and imprisoned many Communist leaders.

- In March 1933, President Hindenburg signed an "Enabling Act" giving Hitler's regime additional powers.
- President Hindenburg died on August 2, 1934. Upon the president's death, Hitler combined the offices of president and chancellor into one office—the fuehrer ("leader") and assumed that office himself.
- These actions completed the transition of Germany from a constitutional republic into a totalitarian fascist state. All this had happened in less than two years (twenty months, to be exact). Germany didn't have another election after the Nazis won a plurality in November 1933 until 1949.
- Hitler did solve Germany's economic difficulties by setting up two versions of currency—one backed by paper only used within the country and another backed by gold and only used outside the country. He got the gold by confiscating the private wealth of an entire category of people—the Jews—enslaving and slaughtering them, using a national history of anti-Semitic racism as his justification.

Also note that the Nazis made great use of the newly developed techniques of propaganda, casting their action to be in the interests of the German workers (the word Nazi is an abbreviation for National Socialist German Workers' Party). In reality, neither extreme was interested in anything but power for themselves.

What happens if a demagogue does gain power? What recourse do people have? For the US, the answer was supposed to be the First Amendment to the Constitution—the (uninfringeable) right to keep and bear arms. This was not some obscure reference to how you maintain a militia. It was to be the last-ditch defense of the people against oppression—mass armed civil disobedience.

In Germany, gangs of ex-military "brownshirts" were used effectively by Hitler to intimidate opponents and squelch any dissent. Here, the use of armed civil disobedience promoted the takeover.

The one time this threat of the use of armed civil disobedience was used in the US resulted in a civil war. Then, the nation had become divided, ideologically, and people of good faith on both sides were unable to prevent that result.

Granted, the issue was a moral one but armed warfare and conquest of the opposition by force did not adequately solve the issue of slavery and left the country with an enduring problem of racism.

The conflict did, however, forever change the nature of the American republic into one with less power to the states and more to the central government. God forbid that violence is ever again used as an attempt to resolve the issue of an ideologically divided populace.

There are alternatives.

One antidote proposed by the founding fathers was to use education to dispel the ignorance all are born with. We now have the publicly funded education system that Thomas Jefferson proposed but was unable to get funded. That system will help as long it is not ideologically compromised and becomes just another element of the partisan divide of the country.

A free press was considered an important check to the threat of takeover of the government by a demagogue presenting false information to the voters. The theory was that the papers that were most reliable would be rewarded by that recognition due to the competitive nature of the business and papers competing for customers. Unfortunately, the massive changes in information technology mean that the press, in a narrow sense, no longer controls the information to the voters. The country needs a modern, trustworthy information system. The core concern—to prevent propagandizing the voters—remains valid.

The threat of a military coup or violence was met by having the president also be the commander in chief of the military (to deal with the threat of violence), have each military officer swear allegiance to the Constitution (and not the president), and set up the military justice system to punish those who violated their oath of allegiance.

This has been very effective in the past, but members of the military are obliged to carry out all "lawful" orders or be subject to court-martial. The more confusion exists about what is constitutional, the less preventive power there is in such an oath. The court at the Nuremberg trials after World War II held that military officers are not protected against being liable for their actions by saying they were "just obeying orders" when they participate in crimes against humanity.

The scarcity of labor problem was the thorniest moral issue when the republic was founded. It was not solved. Provisions were made to outlaw the importing of any new slaves, and the navy was charged with enforcing this law but it was a challenge. Slave-running, like the importation of illegal drugs and aliens today, was an incredibly profitable business.

To the North and West were free states, with yeoman farmers with large families to provide the labor. This was in direct competition with the slave labor used for that purpose in the

South. The result was a civil war and the Fourteenth Amendment to the Constitution. The political response that blunted the effect of that amendment was to have the US Supreme Court rule that racism was okay as long as it was separate but equal, in Plessy v. Ferguson in 1896.

This remains a problem, however. It has been eased somewhat by the mechanization of farming with tractors and other machinery but more often than not, any gains from technology are absorbed by the profit incentive of capitalism (i.e., the monetary gains go into increased profits rather that better wages). Another solution (but also driven by the profit motive) is outsourcing labor to foreign countries. In this way, you shift the oppression to the people of those countries and pocket the gains resulting from not having to use more costly US labor. If not properly checked, the result will be the transformation of the US into a third-world country—a ruling privileged elite, a massive number of poor, and no middle class. A broad solution to immigration that the majority of the populace can assent to is sorely needed, but progress is powerfully opposed by those who benefit financially from the status quo.

Another looming problem is that advances in modern information technology have made it so much easier to deliberately misinform the American people, especially when the profits of the companies involved are so immense and there is no effective check on them using their technology for self-serving purposes.

A related threat comes from the incredible advances made over the past decade or so in the ability to control and manipulate people. The technology presents domestic law agencies with the capability to monitor and track vast numbers of citizens. All that stands in the way of this being totally out of control is a variety of inadequate laws that prohibit elements of the government from spying on US citizens, except when justified by court order.

We have seen that court order process abused when it is in the interest of politicians to do so. I'm referring to the so-called FISA warrant abuse issues. The FBI was given access to the technical information collection capability, under the Patriot Act, in order to handle to problem of tracking and monitoring foreign terrorists coming into the country. The FISA warrant process was supposed to keep any abuse of this in check, but it failed.

Now we hear of people labeling political opponents as domestic terrorists. Does this mean there is a threat of the political element of our country using the means of government to track and control anyone who has been designated as a domestic terrorist? Does this mean the 75 million people of the country who voted for Donald Trump are all in danger of being designated domestic terrorists? This is a grave danger to the country and must be checked before it destroys our civil liberties.

There is a final area of our republic that needs attention— our treatment of Indigenous Americans. Competition for land between Indigenous peoples and new immigrants was recognized as a serious problem from the start.

Two solutions were developed—assimilation and the setting aside of large areas under the exclusive sovereignty of Indigenous Americans. Both were incorporated into a treaty framework between the US government and the sovereign five civilized nations.

The alternative was the use of military force, which was the approach often taken after the US Civil War. The government suddenly had large numbers of troops that could be deployed to the West and used to adjudicate differences between the settlers and the Indigenous peoples. That did not work out well. There was much in the way of atrocities on both sides, but the underlying conflict was the unchecked intrusion of white settlers into lands traditionally and legally under tribal sovereignty.

Appendix C of this book details the first of these treaty solutions. It presents the agreement reached under the Treaty of Dancing Rabbit Creek in 1830, between the US federal government and the Mississippi part of the Choctaw nation.

The terms are dramatic. The Choctaw nation agreed to give up its sovereign rights to its lands in Mississippi in exchange for two things.

First, a new area of land in the West is to be forever ceded as being under Choctaw nation sovereignty. This land is most of what today constitutes the state of Oklahoma.

Second, those who choose may remain and become US citizens and will be given sizable land grants (in the area they own and rule). Others may choose to move to the new tribal lands in the West designated for them and the federal government will provide the transportation to do so. None of those promises made to those who stayed behind were permanent.

It seems clear that racism had gradually become out of control in America in the years after the founding of the new republic and this racism was broadly applied against Native Americans as well as against former Black slaves and their descendants. This was fueled by out of control predatory behavior, and was especially effective to denigrate Native Americans with the full support of a president, Andrew Jackson, who seemed to have a deep hatred of those Native Americans.

What happened? Ten thousand Choctaw people walked to the new lands in an ordeal known as the trail of tears. There were serious difficulties in carrying out the benefits promised to those who stayed behind. There's a name for this—treaty violation. There were no enforcement penalties named, so most of the treaty terms were broken. It cheated the Indigenous Americans out of their lands. Today, the Choctaw nation occupies only about 11,000 square miles in the Southeast part of Oklahoma.

This is only one example of the way the US government treated Native Americans. Before he became president, as a major general, Andrew Jackson led US Army forces to militarily defeat the Creek nation and force them into submission to a treaty that removed them to reservation lands in the West.

Once he was elected president, one of his first actions was getting Congress to enact the Indian Removal Act in 1830. This act gave him the authorization to subdue the other Native American tribes of the Southeast by similar treatment. This was not a novel idea. Both Presidents Jefferson and Madison had expressed the desire for Native American removal to the West but made no attempt to make it happen. However, in a sense, they thought it would be a safe refuge for Native Americans because of their belief that it would be a long time (maybe a century or two) for that land to become settled, if ever, because of the size of the land.

Jackson did not have much opposition to his treaty approach from the other tribes of the so-called five civilized nations. Based on the experience of the Creek nation, they realized the alternative would be overwhelming military defeat, one by one, and eventual treaty submission anyway.

This entire policy was intended to illegally and cruelly clear out Native Americans from their homes in the Southeast US so they could be replaced by new European settlers. This was a massive national disgrace carried out by a clearly bigoted president.

A current ethical obligation of the US to "make things right" is clear. This is not only just but prevents the country from becoming morally bankrupt on human rights issues. Otherwise, it loses moral leverage in negotiating treaties with foreign nations. Foreign opponents of a particular treaty can credibly use the Native American example to ague the untrustworthiness of the US in fulfilling its treaty obligations and also supports a convincing argument of US moral hypocrisy on issues of human rights.

About the Author

Suzanne Miller is a versatile multitasker, having pursued careers in religion, science and engineering, and music, shifting from one to another whenever a major roadblock appeared to thwart her progress. She's now retired from science and engineering and is putting her energies into singing and writing.

She grew up in the Southeastern part of Virginia. On her dad's side, her family has been on the American scene since the country's early founding in 1607. On her mom's side, the family immigrated to North Carolina by way of Barbados in the mid-1600s.

About 20 years ago, her family asked her if she would document the histories of both sides of her family. Being a trained scientist and researcher, this presented no particular challenge, just a lot of hard work. The family asked her to find out if all the old stories of the family were true. They were (and then some new ones).

Based on her research, she ended up becoming a member of the Daughters of the American Revolution (DAR) and was elected Regent of the Annapolis, MD, DAR Chapter. She also became a member of the National Society of Colonial Dames of the XVII Century and became the Vice-President of her Maryland State Chapter.

Over the years, she spent a career as a Naval officer, retiring in 1986 as a Commander. She also was deeply involved in Defense and intelligence work both directly for the US Government, as a civilian, as well as being a senior scientist and program manager in the top Aerospace companies of the country. She also ran her own Defense consulting company, Suzanne R. Miller Associates, for ten years. All this gave her a broad perspective on how nations act and interact.

She has an intuitive side to her personality that has served her well all her life. She has "hunches" and has learned to trust them to lead her into new, and tremendously fulfilling areas of knowledge and awareness as she uses facts or "what if" to test the validity of her hunches.

This new book: I am an American, is the result of two things coming together. The first one was completion of a fully documented and referenced history of her family. The second was one of those hunches just mentioned. As she researched family history, she learned how often those people played either prominent roles in or were Involved in pivotal events of American history. Most recently, one of her "hunches" led her to sort out her own mixed ethnicity, which she had previously had been unaware of.

Because of this, she is able to write this book as an overview of much important American history, but do so on a personal, human level. Quite a few of the stories it tells are not well known to the public.

Telling those stories, in that way, allows her to describe not only what happened but why? She hopes just presenting what she found will help fill the current void she sees in people's understanding of history. This should be of particular value to young people, especially young people who identify with different ethnicities than "white". Documented fact can be used to supplant incorrect information, and make forward-looking discussion more productive.

Suzanne was enabled to pursue many of the things she has done in her life by early education in science and engineering. She holds a bachelor's degree in aeronautical engineering from the University of Virginia and a master's degree in engineering administration and applied mathematics from the George Washington University. She completed all the coursework for a doctorate in applied mathematics at that same university before refocusing her attention, after twenty years of marriage, on her increased responsibilities as the newly divorced parent of her two boys. She is a lifelong Episcopalian. In that capacity, she attended three years of Seminary education at the Claremont School of Theology. Even though she was turned down twice for ordination, this education enabled her to spend five glorious years of her life as the Licensed Lay Vicar and Pastoral Care Assistant of a working-class Baltimore parish and provided much material for her later books.

Even so, to her great disappointment she was unable to gain much recognition and support when dealing with the institutions of the Church and the Educational Community comparable to the affirmation she has received from the military, the Intelligence Community, the Defense Department, the Aerospace Industry and Private Industry.

She mentions this with a purpose, without going into the details.

It communicates to young people just starting out in their careers that the world may oppose your personal vision of what you feel called to do. Even if clearly correct, your perspective may not always triumph. You must not let this prevent you from aiming to do the right thing and never giving up just because the going has gotten tough. You handle opposition with clear thinking and adjusting your tactics.

Even so, there's a great difference between giving up and just shifting your emphasis. I tried never to stick around a place where I wasn't making progress. The best way to make progress in a world that undervalues (or may even hate you) is to aim to always have your efforts directly contribute to whatever is important to your superiors—their bottom line. To the extent you are able to do this, your leaving brings harm (of their own making) to those who oppose you while not frittering away your life in a losing situation.

This can take a bit of courage (especially the first time) but your confidence will grow with success and, "What have you got to lose by leaving?" You do this only when your progress has been stymied. Clear thinking is critical, not just acting on a whim. You may be able to return later when the smoke has cleared and there is, once again, a way forward. With apologies to my canine friends, I'm reminded of a saying, "Even a dog learns from pain". Just don't make it personal.

Much evil is predicated on you cooperating and becoming a victim, turning you towards hate. Only your acceptance and agreement can make you a victim, with the damage to your self-esteem that comes from such victimization. Some wonderful words of Booker T. Washington (Author of "Up From Slavery") come to mind, "I will not permit any man to narrow and degrade my soul by making me *hate* him".

There is also a story about Mother Theresa that applies. A visitor to her ministry among the sick, poor and destitute in the streets of Calcutta remarked that there was no way she could succeed, given the staggering need of so many, compared to the limited amount of aid she could provide. He asked, in the face of such reality, how could she go on? Her reply was that, yes, success was not likely but, "I am called to be faithful, not successful". Success or failure was up to God and not something she needed to worry herself about.

You or I may certainly not be a "Mother Theresa" but the same principle applies. We should be cautious in limiting our possibilities for personal fulfillment by discouragement.

In this vein of never giving up, Suzanne's energies are now focused in two areas: singing and writing. Unlike her youthful career of singing for pay at embassy parties and a local bar in Washington, DC, her current singing activities are confined to singing for free in church choirs as well as membership in the internationally acclaimed Episcopal Chorale Society. She has sung with them around the diocese and went with them on international singing tours until the Covid-19 pandemic put an end to in-person singing, for a while.

Instead, she has embraced singing in virtual choirs until the pandemic recedes. Most recently, she sang (with several hundred of her closest friends and acquaintances) with the Stay at Home Choir from Oxford as they performed John Rutter's: Star Carol, with accompaniment by the Royal Philharmonic Orchestra. It has drawn over 30,000 hits on you tube.

She has released two singing albums. The first is, *It Ain't Over 'Till It's Over*. The second is, *Walking in Love: Food for The Journey*.

In addition to this new book, *I Am an American*, she authored three previous books: *Walking in Love: Why and How?*, *Spirituality 202* and *Spirituality 101*, in reverse chronological order.

The latter two are the fruits of her Seminary education while the other is the product of her experience as a lifelong seeker of truth and a pastor.

In the unforgettable words spoken by Sandra Bullock in the movie, *Miss Congeniality II*, I really do want world peace.

US POPULATION[56] BY REGION, 1790–2000

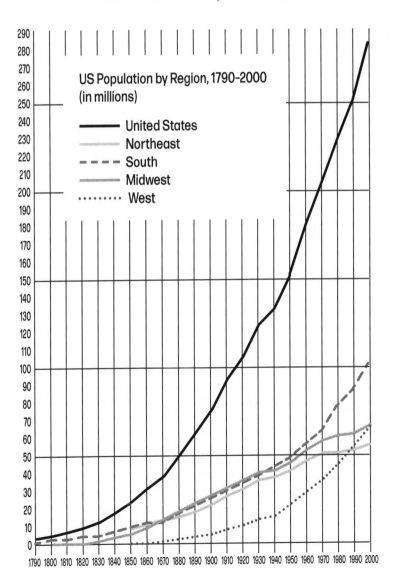

US Population by Region, 1790–2000
(in millions)

—— United States
—— Northeast
- - - South
—— Midwest
········ West

APPENDIX B:

SLAVES TO BARBADOS DOCUMENTATION

I initially wrote Chapter 1, Slaves to Barbados, based on my independent research. Since then I've found out that there's a lot of public dissension and disagreement on the topics of chattel slavery versus indenture, forced labor in the colonies by Scots POWs in America, and the veracity of the atrocities committed against Quakers by both the English as well as the Boston Puritans. This appendix provides documented evidence and citations on these three topics to rebut those accusations without interrupting the flow of the main chapters.

Atrocities Inflicted on Quakers in New England

Let's take the "easiest" one first—the treatment of Quakers by the Boston Colonists. Those atrocities are easily summarized by Figure B-1. That figure is the front cover of a noteworthy book by Edward Burrough. Printed in London in 1662, it was intended to be a sourcebook to back up the appeal for the intervention by King Charles in the New England situation. On this cover, Burrough specifically enumerates the grievances the Quakers were concerned about. I selected this reference because no one would have the audacity to lie in a document written for the king.

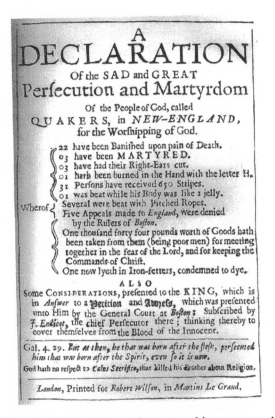

Figure B-1: Front Cover of Edward Burrough's 1662 Book on Quaker Persecution in New England

As to the sentencing by the Boston Court for Quakers to be reduced to chattel slavery, the General Court made a law[57] "that all children and servants and others, that for conscience' sake cannot come to their meetings to worship, and have not estates in their hands to answer the fines, must be sold for slaves to Barbados or Virginia, or other remote parts."

In the execution of this law, here is an excerpt from the court records of the time[58],

"Whereas, Daniel Southwick and Provided Southwick, son and daughter of Laurence Southwick, absenting themselves from the public ordinances, having been fined by the court of Salem and Ipswich, pretending they have no estates, and resolving not to work: The court, upon perusal of a law which was made upon account of debts, in answer to what should be done for the satisfaction of the fines resolves, That the treasurers of the several counties, are and shall be fully empowered to sell the said persons to any of the English nation at Virginia or Barbados, to answer the said fines."

Persecution of Quakers in England

For England itself, here is an excerpt from William Sewells 1695 *History of a People Called Quakers*.[59] At the time of Sewell's publication, the events described occurred in 1661, a little more than thirty years earlier, although it only specifically addresses 4,200 of the prisoners.

"The state of persecution at London, where desperate fury now raged; though it was not in that chief city alone the Quakers were most grievously persecuted: for a little before this time there was published in print a short relation of the persecution throughout all England, signed by twelve persons, showing that more than four thousand and two hundred of those called Quakers, both men and women, were in prison in England; and denoting the number of them that were imprisoned in each county, either for frequenting meetings, or for denying to swear, etc. Many of these had been grievously beaten, or their clothes torn or taken away from them; and some were put into such stinking dungeons, which some great men said, they would not have put their hunting dogs there. Some prisons were crowded full both of men and women, so that there was not sufficient room for all to sit down at once; and in Cheshire sixty-eight persons were in this manner locked up in a small room; an evident sign that they were a harmless people. . ."

There is another good source[60] that describes the situation of Quaker persecution throughout England in detail, by county and locale, covering the 1650 to 1689. This book, titled, *A Collection of the Sufferings of the People Called Quakers*, was published in 1753 in London by Joseph Besse. It is accessible by Google search on the title and its entire contents are available for free, digitally, for the reader.

Quakers Sentenced to Be Transported to Barbados

As to the sentencing of Quakers to be transported to Barbados, here are excerpts from a few still-existing English records[61] I found:

"Majestie hath appointed severall Masters of Ships to carry some of the Quakers now remayning in Newgate, adjudged to be transported to his Majesties Plantations according to the Liste hereunto annexed, It was this day Ordered by his Majestie in Councill, That the Lord Chief Justice of the Kings Bench do forthwith give directions to the Sheriffs of London to cause the respective Numbers of the said Quakers adjudged to be transported, to be forthwith delivered on board the said severall ships taking a Recognizance under the hands of the respective Masters for the safe custody of the said Quakers, and delivery of them to the Governors of the severall Plantations whether [sic] they are bound.

A Liste of the names of the Masters of Ships bound to the Plantations, to transport Convicted Quakers

Jamaica Merchant, William Gainsford Master, bound for Jamaica, is to carry Three Quakers

John and Thomas, John Ceely Master, bound for the Barbados, is to transport Six Quakers

Amity of London, Francis Appleby Master, bound for Mevis [sic], is to transport Seven Quakersss

[The Officers and Farmers of the Customs are directed to allow these vessels to proceed as soon as they are satisfied that each has embarked its due contingent of Quakers.

Instructions are given to the Governors of Nevis, Jamaica and Barbados to receive the transported Quakers, and to employ such as servants in the plantation of them as did not defray the cost of their own transportation. All are to be detained for a space of seven years.]

[On the 15th sixty Quakers now in Newgate adjudged to be transported are ordered to be handed over by the Sheriff of London to William Fudge, master of the Black Eagle of London, a ship of about one hundred tons burden, manned by a master, eight mariners and a boy, to be conveyed to Jamaica, on the same conditions as in the previous order. The usual orders are issued for freeing the vessel from restrictions and for the redemption of the Quakers by the governor of Jamaica.]

[Similar orders are given for the transportation of 50 Quakers to barbados in the John and Sarah of London, a ship of 100 tons burden, John Limbrey Master.]

5 July 1665"

Chattel Bondage Versus Indenture

Chattel bondage is clear—the person is deprived of his or her status as a human being with rights, and becomes a piece of property. All the children born to a female slave are considered slaves from their birth. Under the time's English law, it was illegal to reduce a free person to chattel bondage. The American colonies, however, were not subject to the laws of parliament until the overthrow of King Charles I, although they were under the same queen or king and also tended to use English common law. This was why the Massachusetts courts felt free to convict people to chattel slavery, and why the English Quakers had to appeal directly to the king, not to parliament.

There was this enormous demand for labor in the new colonies. In England, there was a law principle, however, that allowed a person to have a sponsor pay for their transportation expense to a new life in the colonies. In exchange, the person committed to serve for seven years laboring under the sponsor who paid their cost of passage. Theoretically, after that time, the indentured person was to be provided with a suit of clothes, given a shilling, and set free. The law principle was an "innovative interpretation" of common law regarding debts.

In many cases this was a subterfuge. You could rid the jails of their Quaker human cargo as a legal punishment and use the laws of indenture to forcibly transport them—men, women, and children—to a distant land. In the Quaker's case, their "price" was determined when they reached Barbados and auctioned off. Theoretically, the purchaser was only buying seven years of the person's service. In reality, though, in Barbados an indentured worker was included along with chattel slaves, livestock, and furniture as an owner's property, and could be bought and sold. They could also be whipped. And an owner had no obligation to keep together those who were married, but indeed could sell any of the persons and break up the family.

The life expectancy for a laborer in Barbados (either chattel or indentured) was only about seven years due to the harsh conditions of their servitude. Most people never made it to their freedom day. There is a telling account of working conditions in Barbados from a celebrated case of two English Royalists, Marcellus Rivers and Oxenbridge Foyle, who, in 1659 were transported to Barbados because they had allegedly participated in a failed Royalist plot.[62] In 1659 they petitioned parliament for their freedom "on behalf of themselves and three-score and ten more free-born Englishmen sold uncondemned into slavery." The petitioners found Barbados a "place of torment" where they suffered the "most insupportable captivity."

Although the petition was debated at length in parliament, it was denied because parliament was mainly concerned with "the lack of due process" in sending the prisoners to Barbados, "not the fact that they had been sold and were working on plantations."[63]

To me, the end result was that the differences between chattel bondage and indentured bondage, in Barbados, seem trivial. The greatest difference between the two was the hereditary nature of chattel bondage, but this difference disappears as the laboring conditions were lethal over the span of a decade or less. In practical terms, the West African chattel slaves might have been treated better or had a better fate than the indentured slaves. The Quakers were already in prison for quite a while in England, and were not used to heat and little water, while the West African Slaves (at least the ones who survived the voyage) were much younger and sturdier.

It is illuminating that, currently, the US State Department, Office to Monitor and Combat Trafficking in Persons, defines slavery as including sex trafficking, child sex trafficking, forced labor, bonded labor or debt bondage, domestice servitude, forced child labor, or unlawful recruitment and use of child soldiers.[64]

This captures the essence of slavery, which consists of being compelled to perform activities you do not wish to perform—especially when this involved being transported to a foreign land against your will, having no option to leave, and being totally dependent on your overseers for food, shelter, clothing, and survival. In many ways, they held life or death in their hands. There are a multitude of such types of situations by which oppressors gain and enforce such behavior on those subjugated. To say slavery is only traditional chattel bondage is too simplistic. In Barbados, regardless of category, you were a piece of property, you were subject to violent punishment by your master, and had little likelihood of survival.

In summary, from a broader perspective, here is what I conclude on this topic.

The laws of England did not allow a free person to become a chattel slave. At the same time, though, there was an intense demand for labor in the then-new world of America. The English laws regarding indenture were derived from a liberal interpretation of the law relating to people who did not pay their debts. They were subject to imprisonment until and unless their debts were paid.

Definition of the indenture laws allowed a way to meet the demand for laborers in America. A free person could, by their own free will, indenture themselves in order to have an opportunity for a new life in America. When the system was working properly, a person of means would pay the cost of their transportation and the person, in essence, sold seven years of their labor to the purchaser in exchange for the "fare" to America. The king or queen, however, theoretically owned all the land in the American colonies and would customarily give an investor a grant of forty acres of land in exchange for each person the investor "sponsored" to become a colonist. This was how the king or queen generated revenue from their direct "ownership" of the colony—they pocketed the difference between the monies paid on the block in Barbados, minus the cost of shipping. The grant of land to the "sponsor" incentivized them to participate.

In fact, the system often worked well, although it was a grim deal for the laborer. Between the hardships of the voyage itself, upon arrival the working conditions were grueling. In the fourth chapter of this book I mentioned one of my forbears, Nicholas Granger, who was one of one hundred homeless teenage children taken off the streets of London under the vagrancy laws and sent, without choice, to provide free labor in the new colony of Virginia. Only Nicholas and one other survived the ordeal.

Over the years, a variety of laws (or no laws) were used to convict and transport people to Barbados. The previously mentioned Rivers and Foyle case is a perfect example—a total absence of due process to prosecute a political offense again the Puritan rulers. Is it any wonder that by the next year (1660) those high-handed Puritan rulers in England were overthrown?

It has been alleged that any attempt to put indenture in the same context as chattel slavery is "white racism" propaganda to downplay the evils of slavery and deny the descendants of Black chattel slaves their rights to reparations for the evils done to them, when there was no comparison with respect to hardship. One highly respected source[65] says, "the 'white slavery' narrative stresses a sense of shared victimization; this sentiment then serves to discredit calls for reparations from the descendants of enslaved Africans in the United States and the former British West Indies."

I do not think this line of argument is universally true. At its best, indenture was a way for desperately poor persons to move upward in life—to take a risk of losing one's life in the hope of gaining a new life.

For some, the risk paid off, when they were placed in a less oppressive environment but, even then, their lives were never a walk in the park, even under the best of conditions. For others, like those sent to Barbados, they seem to be treated as harshly as their chattel slave co-laborers. There, the system was used to gain cheap labor and work it to death. Barbados law governed their life and the evidence seems to show the system was corrupt. Even though escape was difficult, an "escaped indentured servant" was hunted down under the same laws that applied to fugitive slaves.

Scottish Prisoners of War Indentured to Barbados

Now for the last topic—the use of Scottish prisoners of war indentured to Barbados during the periods under discussion in this book.

They were, indeed, transported against their will to Barbados (and other parts of America) according to the excellent paper[66] of this subject by Gary Cummins. That paper indicates this was done under the authority of the English parliament. In a sense, this was applied in terms of English law, so their enforced labor was considered a form of indenture with a period of seven to ten years.

In the article from *The Scotsman* discussed in the main text of Chapter 1, on the return to Scotland of descendants of these soldiers, it appears that most of the descendants were from Massachusetts. For those POWs sent to Massachusetts, they labored in the iron works—a hot, dirty, dangerous, and unpleasant workplace—but they were in Massachusetts. Unlike the Quakers sent there, however, the Scots POWs were likely well treated and released from service at the end of their enlistments. Such Scots would have been considered respected, good Protestant Christians by the Puritans, and would have been able to settle into a free new life there after their release.

One of the most damning records on this topic that still exists from the British archives has a former Royalist officer, as soon as royal rule was restored in 1660 under the Stuart King Charles II, petitioning the state for money to bring back thirty of his former soldiers from slavery in Barbados. Lieutenant Colonel Thomas Hunt, immediately upon the Restoration, petitioned the government for money to transport home thirty of his soldiers "now in slavery in Barbadoes (sic) whither they were sent by the late powers.[67]

A Lieutenant Colonel would have been in command of a battalion of 150–200 men. By the time they were released, thirty survivors would likely have been the remnant of a significant part of the battalion surrendering and being sent to Barbados.

It is unlikely that any of the Scots POWs sent to Barbados fared any better than any of their Quaker compatriots. Like the Quakers, they would have been treated the same as any indentured laborer, to be exploited and oppressed for English economic interests. This is why the Scots would have joined with their Quaker co-sufferers in colonizing North Carolina after they were released by the Barbados authorities.

THE TREATY OF DANCING RABBIT CREEK

Synopsis of Treaty of Dancing Rabbit Creek, 1830

Article 14 is the most important part of the treaty. Here it is, in full.

ART. XIV. Each Choctaw head of a family being desirous to remain and become a citizen of the States, shall be permitted to do so, by signifying his intention to the Agent within six months from the ratification of this Treaty, and he or she shall thereupon be entitled to a reservation of one section of six hundred and forty acres of land, to be bounded by sectional lines of survey; in like manner shall be entitled to one half that quantity for each unmarried child which is living with him over ten years of age; and a quarter section to such child as may be under 10 years of age, to adjoin the location of the parent. If they reside upon said lands intending to become citizens of the States for five years after the ratification of this Treaty, in that case a grant in fee simple shall issue; said reservation shall include the present improvement of the head of the family, or a portion of it. Persons who claim under this article shall not lose the privilege of a Choctaw citizen, but if they ever remove are not to be entitled to any portion of the Choctaw annuity.

The following are the subjects covered by of each of the treaty articles.

1. Perpetual peace and friendship.
2. Lands (in what is now Oklahoma) west of the Mississippi River to be conveyed to the Choctaw Nation.
3. Lands east of the Mississippi River to be ceded and removal to begin in 1831 and end in 1833.
4. Autonomy of the Choctaw Nation (in Oklahoma) and descendants to be secured from laws of U.S. states and territories forever.
5. U.S. will serve as protectorate of the Choctaw Nation.
6. Choctaw or party of Choctaws part of violent acts against the U.S. citizens or property will be delivered to the U.S. authorities.
7. Offenses against Choctaws and their property by U.S. citizens and other tribes will be examined and every possible degree of justice applied.
8. No harboring of U.S. fugitives with all expenses to capture him or her paid by the U.S.
9. Persons ordered from Choctaw Nation.
10. Traders require a written permit.
11. Streams will be free for Choctaws, U.S. post offices will be established in the Choctaw Nation, and U.S. military posts and roads may be created.
12. Intruders will be removed from the Choctaw Nation. U.S. citizens stealing Choctaw property shall be returned and offender punished. Choctaw offending U.S. laws shall be given a fair and impartial trial.
13. U.S. agent appointed to the Choctaws every four years.

14. Choctaws may become U.S. citizens and are entitled to 640 acres (2.6 km2) of land (in Mississippi) with additional land for children.
15. Lands granted to the Choctaw chiefs (Greenwood LeFlore, Musholatubbee, and Nittucachee) with annuities granted to each of them.
16. Transportation in wagons and steamboats will be provided at the costs of the U.S. Ample food will be provided during the removal and twelve months after reaching the new homes. Reimbursements will be provided for cattle left in Mississippi Territory.
17. Annuities to Choctaws to continue from other treaties. Additional payments after removal.
18. Choctaw Country to be surveyed
19. Lands granted to I. Garland, Colonel Robert Cole, Tuppanahomer, John Pytchlynn, Charles Juzan, Johokebetubbe, Eaychahobia, and Ofehoma.
20. Improve the Choctaw condition with education. Provide tools, weapons, and steel.
21. Choctaw warriors who marched and fought in the army of U.S. General Wayne during the American Revolution and Northwest Indian War will receive an annuity.
22. Choctaw delegate on the floor of the U.S. House of Representatives.

Note the special mention of Choctaw warriors who served with General Wayne as scouts during the American Revolution and later as soldiers during the Northwest Indian War.

On September 26, 1855, Moses Dyer wrote to Choctaw Indian Agent Douglas Cooper on behalf of his stepmother, Ish-tem-ah for his father Ish-kuna-lubbe's last pension payment of $8.46. Ish-kuna-lubbe, whose name translates to "disembowel[s] and kills," was the last living Choctaw scout who served with U.S. General "Mad" Anthony Wayne.

Notes

Preface
1. President Abraham Lincoln, Gettysburg Address, November 19, 1863.
2. President Abraham Lincoln, Annual Message to Congress, December 1, 1862.

Introduction
3. Patrick Henry speech to the Second Virginia Convention of patriots on March 23, 1775, at St. John's Church in Richmond, Virginia.

Overview
4. Carl E. Sigmond, *English Quakers campaign for freedom of religion, 1647–1689*, Global Nonviolent Action Database, 2012. https://nvdatabase.swarthmore.edu/content/english-quakers-campaign-freedom-religion-1647-1689
5. Elisabeth Ritchie, *What were the Scots doing in Barbados and how did they get there? The Ritchies in Edinburgh and beyond*, Wednesday, 12 June 2013, https://ritchiesinedinburgh.blogspot.com/2013/06/what-were-scots-doing-in-barbados-and.html
6. Ibid.
7. James E. Doan, *How the Irish and Scots Became Indians: Colonial Traders and Agents and the Southeastern Tribes*, New Hibernia Review, 3:3 (Autumn, 1999) 9–19.
8. Virginia M. Meyer and John Frederick Dorman, *Adventurers of Purse and Person, 1607–1624/25*, 3rd edition, (Richmond: The Dietz Press, 1987) 322–323.

CHAPTER 1
9. Chris Dolan, *Barbado'ed: Scotland's Sugar Slaves*, 26 April 2009, https://www.bbc.co.uk/programmes/b00k7t42
10. Alison Campsie, *Relatives of Scots soldiers shipped abroad in 17th Century to 'come home' and honour ancestors*, The Scotsman, August 1, 2019
11. Elisabeth Ritchie, *What were the Scots doing in Barbados and how did they get there? The Ritchies in Edinburgh and beyond*, Wednesday, 12 June 2013 https://ritchiesinedinburgh.blogspot.com/2013/06/what-were-scots-doing-in-barbados-and.html

12. Great Britain, Public Record Office, Calendar of State Papers, Domestic, of the Reign of Charles II, Vol. I (1660–1661), 87, 320.

13. Richard S. Dean, *The Barbados Census of 1680: Profile of the Richest Colony in English America*, William and Mary Quarterly Vol.26, No. 1 (Jan 1969), 30.

14. Ibid, 26.

CHAPTER 2

15. Martin Kelly, *The Founding of The North Carolina Colony and Its Role in the Revolution*, ThoughtCo, October 30, 2020, 48.

16. Lindley S. Butler, *Early Settlement of Carolina: Virginia's Southern Frontier*, Virginia Magazine of History and Biography, Vol 79 (Jan. 1971) 28.

17. John Robert Bent Hathaway, ed., *The North Carolina Historical and Genealogical Register*, (Edenton,1901–1903,) III, 146

18. *Quaker Marriage Certificates, Pasquotank, Perquimans, Piney Woods and Sutton Creek Monthly Meetings*, compiled by Gwen Boyer Bjorkman, (Bowie, MD: Heritage Books, 1988), 93

19. *Index to North Carolina Wills, 1665–1900* (Broderbund Software, 2000), 127

20. James E. Doan, *How the Irish and Scots Became Indians: Colonial Traders and Agents and the Southeastern Tribes*, New Hibernian Reviews, Vol3, No.3, Autumn, 1999, 9–19.

21. Chris Dolan, *Barbado'ed: Scotland's Sugar Slaves*, 26 April 2009, https://www. bbc.co.uk/programmes/b00k7t42

CHAPTER 3

22. *An Abstract of North Carolina Wills, 1760–1800, Wayne County*. Will of Joshua Davis, wife Huldah, children: John, Joshua, Richard, Rachel. (Broderbund Software, 2000), 319

23. *State Records of North Carolina*, Vol. XVI, Ed. Walter Clark, (Wilmington: Broadfoot, 1994), 1045. Also Vol XVII, 1059

24. *Marriages in Contentnea Quarterly Meeting of Friends North Carolina Yearly Meeting 1737–1891*, Ed. Theodore Perkins, (Greensboro: Guilford County Genealogical Society, 1988), 187–188.

25. *State Records of North Carolina, Vol. XVII*, Ed. Walter Clark, (Wilmington: Broadfoot, 1994), 206. Also Vol XVI, 1048.

26. Ibid.

27. *Genealogy of Virginia Families*, Indexed by John Winterbottom, (Baltimore: Genealogical Publishing Co., Inc.1981. Vol. V) 235.

28. *An Ordinary of Scottish Arms*, 44.

29. *Genealogy of Virginia Families, Vol. V*, 249.

30. *The Ancestors and Descendants of John Rolf, with Notes on Some Connected Families. The Fleming Family (Concluded)*, The Virginia Magazine of History and Biography, Vol. 24, No. 4 (Oct. 1916), 441.

31. *Encyclopedia of American Quaker Genealogy, 1607–1943, Vol.1 – North Carolina*, 313

32. Ibid. April 26, 1798. Outland, Charity, daughter of Cornelius, Wayne Co. marries John Davis at Turner's Swamp Meeting House.

33. https://forebears.io/surnames/outland#place-tab-2014
34. https://genealogyadventures.net/2016/02/18/
    quakers-slavery-50-shades-of-grey-and-then-some/
35. https://genealogyadventures.net/2016/02/21/
    me-quaker-manumissions-and-an-1828-voyage-to-liberia/

CHAPTER 5
36. *An Act Relating to The Parishes and Congregations of The Protestant
    Episcopal Church in the District of Columbia, Private Law 91−220*, 84
    Stat.2104, 1970.
37. David A. Carrillo and Shane G. Smith, *California Constitutional Law: The
    Religion Clauses*, University of San Francisco Law Review, Vol.45, Winter,
    2011), 689 - 777

CHAPTER 6
38. https://www.census.gov/history/www/genealogy/decennial_census_
    records/censuses_of_american_indians.html
39. By Rob (talk) - Own work (Original text: self-made), Public Domain, https://
    commons.wikimedia.org/w/index.php?curid=10531936
40. 1 Stat. 103, enacted March 26, 1790
41. *The 10 greatest controversies of Winston Churchill's career.* BBC News. 26
    January 2015.
42. The Choctaws, Creeks, Cherokees, Chickasaws, and Seminoles.
43. https://www.choctawnation.com/choctaw-nation-oklahoma
44. https://en.wikipedia.org/wiki/
    List_of_Indian_reservations_in_the_United_States

CHAPTER 7
45. Henry Louis Gates, Jr., DNA Testing: Review, African American Lives,
    reviewed in About.com, https://web.archive.org/web/20090313231943/
    http://racerelations.about.com/od/ahistoricalviewofrace/a/dnaandrace.
    htm
46. Angela Saini, Superior: The Return of Race Science, Beacon Press, Fourth
    Estate Books, 2019
47. https://www.nhm.ac.uk/discover/cheddar-man-mesolithic-britain-blue-
    eyed-boy.html
48. Nina G. Jablonski, Living Color, The Biological and Social Meaning of Skin
    Color, University of California Press, 2104.
49. Du Bois, W.E.B., Black Reconstruction in America, 1860−1880, Free Press,
    1999. First published in 1935.
50. Kim Parker, Juliana M. Horowitz, Rich Morin, Mark H. Lopez, Pew Research
    Center, *Multiracial in America: Proud, Diverse and Growing in Numbers*,
    Washington, DC, June, 2015.
51. Henry Louis Gates, Jr., "Michelle's Great-Great-Great-Granddaddy—and
    Yours." *The Root.com*, 8 October 2009.
52. Esteban J. Parra, (1998). "Estimating African American Admixture
    Proportions by Use of Population". The American Journal of Human

Genetics. 63 (6): 1839–1851. doi:10.1086/302148. PMC 1377655. PMID 9837836.

CHAPTER 8

53. Special Field Orders No. 15, a wartime order proclaimed by Union General William Tecumseh Sherman on January 16, 1865

54. Robert E. Galeman, *Gross National Product in the United States, 1834–1909*, National Bureau of Economic Research, 1966, 8, http://www.nber. org/chapters/c1565

55. Gildas, *De Excidio et Conquestu Britanniae* (On the Ruin and Conquest of Britain), 510–530 AD.

APPENDIX A

56. US Census Bureau: https://www.census-charts/Population/ pop-us-1790-2000.html

APPENDIX B

57. George Bishop, *New England Judged, by The Spirit of The Lord*, 1661, 88.

58. Ibid, 96.

59. William Sewell, *History of a People Called Quakers*, 1695, Book Two, 2.

60. Joseph Besse, *A Collection of the Sufferings of the People Called Quakers*, London, 1753.

61. Acts of the Privy Council of England: Colonial Series, Vol. 1, AD 1613–1680 (Liechtenstein: Kraus Reprint Ltd., 1966) First Published London: HMSO, 1908. 388, 393–394, 402, 414, 415.

62. Marcellus Rivers, *Englands Slavery or Barbados Mechandize* (sic), Printed in London, 1659, 23 pages.

63. J.S. Handler, & M.C. Reilly, (2017). *Contesting "White Slavery" in the Caribbean, New West Indian Guide / Nieuwe West-Indische Gids*, 91(1–2), 30–55.

64. https://www.state.gov/what-is-trafficking-in-persons/

65. Ibid. Abstract, 1.

66. Gary T.Cummins, *Treatment of prisoners of war in England during the English Civil Wars*, 22 August, 1642 - 30 January, 1648/49 (1968). University of Montana, Graduate Student Theses, Dissertations, & Professional Papers 40.

67. Great Britain, Public Record Office, Calendar of State Papers, Domestic, of the Reign of Charles II, Vol. I (1660–1661) 87, 320.

Made in the USA
Las Vegas, NV
27 April 2022

48082369R00125